An Imperfect Healer

The Gifts of a Medical Life

Larry Kramer, M.D.

Pottersfield Press, Lawrencetown Beach, Nova Scotia,
Canada

Library and Archives Canada Cataloguing in Publication

Title: An imperfect healer : the gifts of a medical life / Larry Kramer.
Names: Kramer, Larry, 1948- author.
Identifiers: Canadiana (print) 20190119810 | Canadiana (ebook) 20190119829 | ISBN 9781988286907 (softcover) | ISBN 9781988286914 (EPUB)
Subjects: LCSH: Kramer, Larry, 1948- | LCSH: Narrative medicine. | LCSH: Physician and patient. | LCSH: Medical care—Canada—Anecdotes.
Classification: LCC RC48 .K73 2019 | DDC 610.69/6—dc23

Cover design: Gail LeBlanc

Pottersfield Press gratefully acknowledges the financial support of the Government of Canada for our publishing activities. We also acknowledge the support of the Canada Council for the Arts and the Province of Nova Scotia which has assisted us to develop and promote our creative industries for the benefit of all Nova Scotians.

Pottersfield Press
248 Leslie Road
East Lawrencetown, Nova Scotia, Canada, B2Z 1T4
Website: www.PottersfieldPress.com
To order, phone 1-800-NIMBUS9 (1-800-646-2879) www.nimbus.ca

Printed in Canada
Pottersfield Press is committed to preserving the environment and the appropriate harvesting of trees and has printed this book on Forest Stewardship Council® certified paper.

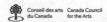

To all those
who have walked through my office door.

Contents

Author's Note 7

Prologue 9

A Quiet Life and A Quiet Death 16

A Kaleidoscope of Patients 22

The OR 27

Tragedy 32

A Christmas Gift 37

An Emergency Room Visit 42

Death and Courage 46

My Son 51

The House Call 57

A Very Human Parade 61

Babies 67

The Victory of Age 72

Thank You 76

The Existentialism of Birds 81

Those On Whom I Depend 86

A Community Hospital 92

Courage 98

Goodbye 105

A Reunion 110

Who Will Whisper Vespers   116

Too Complicated   120

The Prayer Lady, The Bomber Pilot,
    and The Russian Princess   125

God   131

Waste   136

Escape   143

The Beginning of the End   149

Time to Change   154

Friendship   160

Working Abroad   164

The End   171

Contemplating Retirement   176

Internship   180

Summing Up   186

Acknowledgements   188

Author's Note

The physician should not treat the disease but the patient who is suffering from it.

– Maimonides

Medicine has always been more than a job. Too often it becomes a way of life, an all-pervasive reason for being. How far down this road physicians go in defining themselves frequently becomes a problem. Too easily they become etirely and always physicians. This makes for some awfully good clinicians and some awfully poor human beings.

To be a physician is hard enough. It takes so much time and effort that there just isn't energy for very much else. A selection bias seems to exist for those willing to sacrifice everything on the altar of medicine. To survive residency this becomes almost a necessity. Can it be surprising that the individual becomes psychologically welded to his career? Yet any definition of self cannot be so one-dimensional.

We need to see beyond this narrow view. We need to see medicine as a means of understanding and appreciating a far greater picture. Through medical knowledge we address only a piece of the puzzle of what it is to be human. Without a compassionate understanding, knowledge alone is like the proverbial one hand clapping. We must see ourselves in our patients. This might make us not only better physicians, but also more complete human beings.

In bygone days, the art of medicine was paramount. The laying on of hands, the listening, the understanding, the empathy were all we had to offer. Now science has superseded and threatens to eclipse any remaining vestiges of art. The pendulum has swung away from humane interactive medicine towards a colder impersonal science. We are more prone to treat laboratory or X-ray results than we are to care for the broken heart or the defeated spirit these results have produced. And if we do treat that depression, we are more likely to define it in neurochemical terms than in the intangibles of human loss and despair. We will be more likely to use pills than we will be to listen.

Both the art and the science are essential to good medicine. We have perhaps worshipped the science and neglected the art. The perfect doctor is a combination: the scientist who understands the anatomy, physiology, and pathology as well as the artist who appreciates the poetry, the history, the feelings, the personality, the motivations that make each of us uniquely human. The healer considers both and offers help that is scientific, and compassionately human.

Art and science. Apollo and Dionysius. Balance is the key.

Prologue

I was a family doctor in a small Ontario town for twenty-seven years. Just a GP, as my kids used to say. From 1975 until 2002 I worked in a medical clinic across the street from a ballpark. In the summer, through a spacious window in my office, I could watch kids playing baseball whenever I tired of the paperwork piling up on my desk. For the first twenty-five years I loved the life. For the last two, hate would be a kind word. I was burnout defined.

There were three other family docs in the clinic who seemed to be lifers. Many others came and went, stayed a few months, or maybe even a few years, and then left, disaffected by the often cloistered rural lifestyle as well as the frequently challenging medical circumstances. After years of big-city training, the change was, for many, too much.

The four of us had gone to the same medical school, our graduations spread over some eleven years. We could reminisce about med school days and old profs we had in common. Maybe this made us think alike. We did what most small town GPs of that era did – too much and everything.

A local hospital was the setting for delivering babies, covering the ER, rounding on in-patients, doing minor surgeries, assisting at major ones, giving anaesthetics, and meeting for coffee nearly every morning in the doctor's lounge. Sadly, and perhaps by way of necessary evolution, most of these activities for family physicians have disappeared, including the doctor's lounge.

This hospital was, for most of us, ninety percent of our problems and ten percent of our income. But working there was what we felt obliged to do. We were trained largely in hospitals and were comfortable there. And in a small town, at least from a medical perspective, if you didn't do it, it probably wouldn't get done. Patients would at the very least be inconvenienced (it was a long trip into the city) and at worst they would be put at risk. So mornings were generally spent at the hospital while afternoons and some evenings were spent in the office. Nights too often were spent in the ER or on call for the clinic or anaesthesia. And babies arrived on their own schedule.

Realistically, in a small town, you were never off call. Being on call became the norm as did being at home less and less. I recall never thinking much about it then. I had been well conditioned by the professional expectations that were ingrained in medical school, internship, and residency. These were both subtle (Q: What's wrong with taking call one night in two? A: You miss half the good cases.) and obvious (the surgeon whom I never saw out of OR greens in four years of medical school). How could I behave otherwise?

The nurses at the hospital were often friends who knew where you lived and called you by your first name. They knew that, for your patients, it was much easier to deal with someone who was familiar with the problems. A phone call was easy. It's hard to fault their logic and I never learned how to say "no." Physician quality of life wasn't a priority then. Medicine was my lifestyle. And I basked in the false bravado of its glow. I just didn't know yet what I had bought into.

I worked hard. I loved it. At least that's how it was at first. But this kind of single-mindedness eventually extracts a price. Kids' dance recitals, graduations, and birthdays weren't so much forgotten as they were pre-empted by a delivery, or being on call, or having to work the ER or anaesthesia. Spouses weren't ignored as much as they were taken for granted. It was all too easy to do. So for twenty-five years I managed, trying to be all things to all people. As a partner, father, physician, colleague, confessor, non-complainer, and on-call masochist I both succeeded and failed.

At first life was good. I was doing what I enjoyed and getting paid way more than I ever imagined possible. My partner, Clare, and I were young, prosperous, respected, even pedastalled (if that is a word). My family grew to three kids and we seemed to be living the dream. But the carousel spun ever faster. It became difficult to hold on. There wasn't enough of me for all the bits of life that were demanding a piece. Children grew up quickly. I didn't notice. Parents aged. Again, too busy to notice. Material things now seem a poor replacement for all the things I never had time to do.

Eventually I realized I had to get out. My coping strategies, short of leaving, never seemed to help for long. Holidays were yearned for and dreaded. The preparation, arranging calls and coverage of patients with colleagues who were already overloaded, and then returning to work piled up, was daunting. It was easier not to go. Locums at a slightly different type of work – as a GP in a large psych facility – ironically, brought a temporary measure of sanity to my world. But the comfort was always short-lived. By year twenty-six the stress, depression, and anxiety never really left. Medicine was always on my mind. There was little room for anything else.

It is possible to carry on in this fashion for many years, even a lifetime. But it is very hard to do so without losing a part of yourself along the way. Some of us became welded to our careers, addicted to our patients. Work became our reason for being. Some couldn't change the work so they changed what they could. New families and new friends might be more forgiving. Still others looked for solace in the chemistry of drugs or alcohol. A few found a balance. Medical culture, then more than now, was less ready to accept this solution. It preferred sacrifice and a willing, even eager, victim.

After a few years, when the novelty and lustre of practising medicine had worn off a bit, I began noticing what wonderful stories my patients had to tell. Mostly these were not told in words but in the fabric of their lives. Given the privileged, almost priestly, position doctors (particularly in small towns) held, I had access to the most intimate details and complications of their lives. Compelling stories abounded. They were funny and sad, tragic and joyful. I found writing them down helped me to cope with both their lives and mine. And they taught me so much: a little bit about medicine, a lot about myself, and a great deal about life in general.

In 2002 I reached the end of my tolerance. I could no longer be all things to all people. I left my small town to become a "hospitalist" in a nearby larger centre. There, my practice would be limited to adult, hospital in-patients – those who had no family physician or whose family physician no longer had hospital privileges. The scope of what I needed to know was more limited. Goodbye obstetrics and paediatrics. Paperwork wasn't a whole lot less, just different. My hours (forty hours a week, on paper) sounded better than they actually were, since you simply stayed until the work was done, and the call schedule (about one night in two weeks and one weekend a month, depending how many were away on holidays) was a relief. I actually had time to talk to patients, and to think about and research their problems. It was paradise for a while.

As cutbacks continued to mount, our patient population began to suffer from what a colleague fondly dubbed "acuity creep." They were demographically older, more acutely ill on admission, on more drugs, and had more co-morbidities. Help was also harder to find. Tertiary centres were overcrowded and our own consultants were overworked. After nearly ten years I found myself in much the

same position as when I had left general practice –
longer and longer hours, more and more call, and
worrying to the point of insomnia about patients
I couldn't help and for whom I could find no help
when they needed it most. It was time to leave again.

For the last three years of my career I worked
part-time as a locum physician. It was like being a
grandparent, all the fun and few of the headaches.
I could always give the patient the option of coming back to see the "real doctor" in a few weeks'
time. He/she would know their situations so much
better than I could. This was an out for both the patient and myself. And then, after forty years, even
this couldn't keep me interested. I decided to retire
before my "best by" date or maybe after it. Who can
ever know?

That's where I am now and it has its own chal-
lenges. I feel like I should still be working, that I
have let the side down. Although this feeling is fading with the passage of time, I think it will persist
like an instinct dulled by conscious effort. And I've
begun to write down some new stories as well as
to rewrite and revise some old ones. Once again it's
been therapeutic, easing me gently into this phase of
my life. Interesting that at nearly seventy years old I
can still be having phases.

The Medical Post – a nationwide newspaper for
physicians – has been kind enough to publish most
of these pieces over the last forty years. In truth,
the stories and people are largely composites, not
drawn from one person alone. They are a pastiche of
those I encountered along the way. And also in truth,
I can no longer recall by name most of the patients

in these stories. They were never identified by name and now I remember only their faces. Many were elderly when I originally wrote their stories so many years ago and have long since passed on. There are some I can never forget. I have wanted not so much to convey individual stories as to present a generic view of what lies within us all and to say thank you to those who enriched my life.

Oddly, their stories seem to have become my story, so closely have our lives been intertwined. They serve to remind me of who I once was, what I once did, and how I have passed much of my life. And perhaps, at least in some part, they are the stories of us all.

A Quiet Life and A Quiet Death

Then Old Age, and Experience, hand in hand,
Lead him to Death, and make him understand
— John Wilmot

I never knew him when he wasn't old and frail and small. Almost wizened in appearance, his short stature made him comically gnomish. His hair was almost gone and it exposed ears too large. The skin of his face sagged badly and had that worn wrinkled look of too much sun over too many years. His clothes always seemed overly big, and he wore those heavy one-piece long johns with the funny rear flap all year round. Thick woollen plaid shirts were always tucked neatly into baggy trousers held by a belt with too many notches. He moved with the slow shuffling gait of the aged, and spoke in that polite subdued manner of an era long gone by. Yet he remained bright and alert to the world around him. The sad indignities of old age had mercifully spared him.

I wonder what he was like so many years ago, when youth still graced his form, before the decades left so many memories. I imagine him stocky and muscular, his body made hard by the only work he ever knew, the railroad. It too was now of a bygone time. His stride would have been robust and long, his voice full and unhesitating. He would have been dressed in the fashion of the time and moved with confidence and an easy grace. He may have worn the uniform of the Great War and espoused that naïve idealism of the young and untried. But that was then and this is now. What would that youth think of the old man who sits before me?

He used to come to the office regularly, always accompanied by his wife of over sixty years. She would gush, almost giggle, answers to questions directed at him. Yes, his appetite was good and he didn't have to get up too often at night, and his bowels were regular, and his arthritis wasn't too bad and he tried to be active every day, and he took his medication regularly. In contrast he gave concise, unadorned answers. "Yes," "No," and "Not so bad, Doc" were about as verbose as he ever became.

She seemed to hover about him trying to address his every want. Almost avian was her constant motion, her desire, to attend to him. His well-being, physical and mental, was pretty much entirely dependent on his companion of so many years. She would help to dress him and to feed him, and to clean up after him. Caring of this magnitude could only be driven by a devotion of the purist kind.

They never had any children. It just didn't happen. I have seen others driven apart by this trick of fate. It seemed to make him and his wife need each other more. The love between them was unspoken, yet almost palpable. I wonder if a relationship this grand transcends the power of words, at least mine, and maybe even theirs.

The weight of ninety-three years imposes a lot of hardships on the human body. He suffered from the standard afflictions of age: osteoarthritis, atherosclerotic heart disease, cancer of the prostate, and probably a few others I never knew about. He dealt with them remarkably well, more through genetic luck and the kindness of his lover-wife than modern medicine, I suspect.

None the less I monitored his state of health and prescribed all the routine medications we can't seem to die without – digoxin, a diuretic, occasionally an analgesic, and some Euflex to retard the cancer. I hope they did not shorten his life. I hope they, I hope I, made some difference.

After his last admission to hospital he was too weak to travel very much, so I began to visit him at home. I would drop by unannounced and be afforded a view into yesterday.

Their lives had all the simplicity of an old movie. Faded black and white photographs adorned the walls; young men in uniform posed seriously or laughed recklessly, unaware of their fate. Do they live in someone's memory now? Each day was as much like the next as it was the previous. He would sit in his chair, rarely having the strength to move very much, smoking his pipe, and looking at, if not seeing, the flickering black and white television which seemed to be on all the time. She would move about slowly, bringing him tea, helping him to the bathroom, never far from his side. They would chat aimlessly all the day long. Their lives were predictable, the plot never changed.

The house was old, covered in a kind of gritty tarpaper of a dull and worn green colour that may have been popular fifty years ago. It had the appearance of a home poorly kept, not out of neglect, but simply from an inability to carry out the many chores a house demands. The furniture was antique not by design, but simply because it had survived these many years and had never been replaced. The rooms always seemed dimly lit and had that musty smell of insufficient cleaning and dampness unnoticed. Their two-storey house, once nestled on a quiet street, now stood too close to the asphalt of a busy roadway. It wouldn't be allowed today. So much of the past wouldn't be allowed today.

In the summer I would often find him sitting on a tiny front veranda watching the life of this small community pass by. He always seemed so happy to see me. A quick check of blood pressure, heart, lungs, and a few questions – "How's the water-works?" "Appetite good?" – were necessary, but also, at ninety-three, quite pointless. I doubt that anything I did would provide more than a small measure of comfort.

I longed to ask him the secrets of so long a life. But somehow I felt this would betray our doctor-patient relationship and place him in the uncomfortable position of trying to explain the unexplainable. I doubt that he considered living all that complicated. He had grown old gracefully and accepted each day's rising sun as another victory. Who was I to infer some meaning beyond the obvious? Albert Camus asked, "Why not commit suicide?" I doubt that he ever heard of Albert Camus and if he had, he would have thought him silly. I also doubt he ever had his fifteen minutes of fame and I don't think he cared about that either. I see him sitting before me in triumph, embodying the best of all of us.

As fall moved into winter, he became weaker and could no longer manage the stairs to their bedroom. I think this physical separation from his wife hastened the inevitable. He developed the habit of sleeping downstairs on the couch. When she tired of sleeping in the sofa chair beside him, she would sadly climb the stairs after he had fallen asleep.

On my last visit he looked particularly frail. I could not understand his words and he was too weak to move off the couch. Before I left I took his hand. He squeezed it for a moment longer than a handshake demands and opened his eyes long enough to make eye contact. This was goodbye and thank you. He knew.

His wife called early the next morning and almost apologetically asked if I would come over. He had died during the night. She was upset, but in a controlled, expectant sort of way. She felt badly that she had spent the night upstairs and had not been there at the moment of his passing. She spoke of the good night kiss of the previous evening, how it lingered, and was accompanied by an unexpected and enigmatic smile.

He died at home as he had lived – quietly, simply. I hope I have the good fortune to do the same. His life is a journey we all take. His courage was the courage to go on every day without complaint and with achieving some measure of happiness. I have seen myself, I have seen all of us, in the frail body and bright eyes of this old man. He has traversed some vast sea of time and experience and emerged a victor, simply by going on every day. I've begun to think that life isn't much more complicated than that.

A Kaleidoscope of Patients

Blessed are the poor, for theirs is the kingdom of God.
Blessed are they that mourn, for they shall be comforted.

– Matthew 5:2-3

She never says thank you. Every three or four weeks she comes to my office and asks for medication. She rarely says more. Sh is in her mid-fifties but looks ancient. She has no drug plan and she has no money. Her shoulder hurts so much she can't do the only work her sixth-grade education allows. No physician can find anything very specific wrong with her. Canada Pension Plan has already turned down her request for a disability pension. And, no, I am not making this up, her husband is dying of pancreatic cancer.

I search my cupboard looking for a few weeks' supply of one NSAID (non-steroidal anti-inflammatory drug) or another. I wonder at the hopelessness that is her life. That she doesn't say thank you no longer surprises me. She hasn't much for which to be thankful.

A former prime minister's assistant secretary visited me today. She's a dear lady of ninety-seven, as bright as sunlight and as refreshing as cool water on a summer's day. We speak of a Canada that was: Banff National Park in all its pristine beauty before mega-tourism, clandestine wartime meetings, and names I recognize only from history books. Her prime minister never talked to his dog, "at least not in my presence," and he was quite sane "most of the time." I enjoy her visits tremendously. They are serendipity on dull or overwhelming days.

I listen to her few complaints, more comments really, and monitor the consequences of her age ... a heart that is failing, vision that is almost gone, and joints that reject activity. Yet she remains bright and alive. She enjoys every day, smiles often, and laughs easily. I envy her wisdom of so many years. I admire the tranquillity and courage she brings to living. What is her secret?

Ms. Y has been depressed her whole life. A childhood stained by abuse seems to have set this depression in concrete. No amount of psychotherapy (group and/or individual analysis for over twenty years) or medication seems to have made much difference. ECT (Electroconvulsive Therapy) and institutionalization haven't helped much either.

I can always read her mood as soon as she walks in the door. If an overweight, frumpy, dishevelled, sweat-suit-wearing automaton enters, I know a difficult time is beginning. If she comes as a svelte, confident, well-dressed woman, I know the problems will be easy to solve: appearance as a mirror of the soul.

She continues to visit a psychiatrist, a counsellor at the adult mental health centre, and myself regularly. Lately she has taken to burning herself with cigarette butts. I suspect this creates a pain with which she can deal. Sometimes the futility is overwhelming. I cannot begin to imagine what it must be like from the inside. Empathy ceases to have meaning.

They visit every six weeks or so. They're both in their early eighties and have been married forever. They speak softly and seem genuinely happy with each other. He is legally blind and has chronic obstructive lung disease and a bad heart. She's dying slowly, but cheerfully, with congestive cardiac failure. They are as poor as church mice, but one year they gave me a Christmas card with five dollars in it and apologized that it couldn't be more. I didn't know what to say. Thank you seemed so inadequate.

I renew their medication and occasionally juggle the dose or add something new. Realistically I know my manipulations mean very little. They seem content to be told that the mechanics of living are still there. At the end of every visit he points to a calendar on my wall that he can barely see and squints sharply while he calculates out loud, "Let's see, six weeks will be –" and he fixes an exact date for a return visit. They are kind and gentle people. If I make it to the next life, I'm sure they'll be part of the welcome.

Mr. G is alone and dying. Over one crisis or another, imagined or real, he has alienated his family. Divorced, shunned by his children, he lives an isolated life in a trailer somewhere out in the country. He has an adenocarcinoma that gives him only a few months to live. Yet he steadfastly refuses much help of any kind. Since the diagnosis was made and the prognosis offered, I have seen him but once. He will die as he lived, contrary, stubborn, and alone. I suspect he is very frightened as well. I regret that I have been unable to help him either with his illness or with his fear and loneliness. I must overcome the feeling that his failure is my failure.

The princess visits me far too often. Two or three time a month she graces my office with her presence. She is aristocratic India of the Raj, flowing blue silk sari covered by a snowmobile jacket. Usually she is accompanied by her entourage: a brother, a cousin, a couple of nephews and nieces, all content to be more poorly dressed and to allow her to do the talking, albeit in very broken English. My time with her is usually concerned more with resisting her imperial dictates and requests than diagnosis. She has generally decided on what needs to be done and I am the unimportant but necessary facilitator.

She is culturally out of place and may be generations out of time. But I can only visit her world through the looking glass of my small office and our limited time. I imagine there is so much more: as in medicine, so in life.

B.V.W. is hopelessly dramatic; at every visit she shouts and gestures theatrically. Despite her sixty-seven years, long blonde hair is piled on top of her head while ringlets descend to her shoulders. She is always dressed entirely in black and often wears a cape. I feel as if I should address her as countess. At one time she was a concert cellist in Eastern Europe. But problems within and without led to a psychiatric diagnosis that has defined her in a seemingly irrevocable way. The line between genius and madness is indeed thin.

I wonder why she keeps coming back to see me. I refuse to prescribe the narcotics she so often requests and she refuses to see any more psychiatrists. I see a stalemate. She sees an audience. The performance continues.

These are the people who fill my days and all too often my nights. Increasingly I question my role in their lives. I try to listen and maybe put on a band-aid or two. But I remain in awe at the diversity of their demons and the wonderful complexity of their lives. I have seen courage in the face of death and cowardice in the face of life. I learn often and perhaps occasionally am able to teach a little.

A wise man suggested that medicine should comfort always, help when it can, and harm never. I doubt that I've reached these lofty goals, but I hope that over the years I have given back a small portion of what I have received. Those who come for help bring gifts they cannot imagine. I am wealthy beyond need.

The OR

The wounded surgeon plies the steel
That questions the distempered part;
Beneath the bleeding hands we feel
The sharp compassion of the healer's art
Resolving the enigma of the fever chart.

– T.S. Eliot

The Operating Room is filled with so many ghosts. Sometimes I feel the nearness of all those who have been pulled back from the brink, of all those who have been suspended here in a dreamless anaesthetic sleep. Most only flirt with that other world before returning unscathed, repaired and new again. Their cases are routine, as common as our daily bread. Only a very few begin another journey here. We have operated on their bodies, but what happens to their souls? Do they leave some part of themselves here? What is a soul? Do they even have souls? I never asked these questions when I was working there. Metaphysics is not popular in the OR.

I used to work in the operating room almost every day. There was a certain tension there, an excitement that didn't exist in any other area of the hospital. As a GP-anaesthetist, I enjoyed the adrenalin rush of emergent care, the satisfaction of definitive treatment. It was so uncomplicated.

Now I only visit the OR occasionally, to hold retractors or make conversation during varicose vein strippings. I could be anyone and it is hard to imagine that my presence means very much. My function seems to be almost social: laugh at the jokes, discuss politics, and make a point of being politically incorrect. I am tolerated like a too distant relative who comes infrequently and whose visits must be cordial but not too close. My movements are clandestinely watched by the OR nurses to ensure that I don't violate some rules of sterile technique. They didn't use to watch me so surreptitiously. But now I'm a stranger, an outsider, not to be trusted.

Surgeons are interesting people. I am fascinated by the certainty of their world: *ubi pus, ibi evacuum* (Where there is pus, there evacuate), black and white, to the point. How envious I am of their ability to visualize problems with such absolute clarity, to define answers so clearly, to act so precisely. This capacity seems to extend beyond surgery. Politics, economics, religion, even ethics, seem to be very straightforward, even simple, in the OR. Answers seem obvious here. I feel I've missed something. Preston Manning and Ross Perot are popular in the Operating Room.

But sometimes I see beyond the facade. I see hands that tremble occasionally. I see indecision, a changed mind, uncertainty. I see a surgeon who hums or whistles when things are going badly, as if to assure himself that control will never be lost. I find comfort in these all too human frailties – and strangely, find that they inspire confidence.

My world is rarely so easy. Medically and metaphysically I live in constant doubt. Black and white are colours I rarely see. More often than not, I can make no definite diagnosis of the little old lady in no acute distress, complaining of fatigue not yet diagnosed, or in the medical vernacular, LOL in NAD C/O Fatigue NYD. The endless parade of children all seem to have viral upper respiratory infections (colds), although I can't really prove it. The headaches of unknown aetiology are probably tension ... but it could be a brain tumour, I suppose.

I take refuge in the words of a hopelessly psychotic patient who told me, "Don't wait for that moment of absolute certainty – it never comes. Make a decision and move on." Wise words from an unlikely source.

I generally have no answers for what I thought were complex problems. Much of the time I don't know what's absolutely right or what's wrong. Maybe it depends on the circumstances, maybe absolute doesn't exist ... maybe I simply haven't found the right parameters to measure by, maybe I don't know how to apply those I have ... maybe. But I digress. There is no room for digression in the Operating Room.

Anaesthesiologists always look tired. They seem vaguely anxious and carry a special vigilance that makes them acutely aware of minute details.

Coloured lights, numbers that flash brightly, readouts, printouts, lines in most every orifice measuring most of what is measurable, switches, valves, bells, and whistles preoccupy them. As I watch the guardian of this impressive technical array I wonder who controls whom.

I remember the first anaesthetic I gave, with a blood pressure cuff as the only monitoring device. I am frightened now and think myself lucky to have skated on ice so thin.

Operating Room nurses are strong people. Some are too strong. They are all competence and technology, unmoved by impulse, unable, or afraid, to feel too much. They rarely laugh and they never cry. Some are too soft. Their work overwhelms them. All pain becomes their pain, all suffering becomes their suffering. They also rarely laugh, but they cry too often. They don't last long. Some are the perfect mix of compassion and competence. They function smoothly, professionally. They laugh a great deal and they don't cry until after. I admire them.

The curtain rises every morning at eight o'clock. The players arrive. The surgeon, never like Hamlet, vacillating and unsure, but always looking straight ahead, certain of the truth, is rarely late. The assistant enters to play the foil to the surgeon's straightforward view of the cosmos. Already looking weary, the anaesthetist has begun worrying long before curtain time. The nurses, steadfast and ready, are the foundation on which this play is built. Only the patient and the plot change, and those almost hourly. The theatre of the real is about to begin.

Memory is too often a flawed reflection of the past. Jaded by wishes of what might have been, I suspect that it sometimes gives me what I want to remember, rather than what was. Triggered by the strangest stimuli, I find myself subliminally wandering back to the OR.

Colours. Colours take me back. Red is too obvious, but I remember how it elicited both fear and hope. I remember the green everyone wore – so clean, so full of innocence every morning, so crimson stained and tired every night. I remember the soft blue of the sky I watched from my windowsill perch only a few feet yet many miles from the anaesthetic machine that ran my life. I remember the warmth of the sun through that window and the longing I felt to be elsewhere. I remember the tepid, thick slaughterhouse smell of an open abdomen, the repugnant stench of pus left too long, the happy smell of vernix and clean amniotic fluid.

Part of me misses being there, misses the drama, the excitement. But a larger part realizes that I really can't go home again. Home has changed. I have changed. I am physically unmotivated and metaphysically uninterested. Yet the fascination remains and probably always will. I remember a surgeon telling me that when asked what his religion was, he replied, "Surgeon." I think I understand now.

Tragedy

Bid me despair and I'll despair,
Under that cypress tree:
Or bid me die, and I will dare
E'en Death, to die for thee.

– Robert Herrick

They looked like everyone's grandparents should look. She was slight and stooped. A kerchief always covered her snow-white hair and was tied beneath her chin in an old-world fashion. A long, straight, shapeless dress was pillared by baggy nylons with a seam up the back. She shuffled and wore bifocals, while the weight of eighty-three years made her seem smaller than she was. Her life had been immigrant hard: a stereotypical arrive-with-nothing-and-build-a-new-life struggle. Until one or two years ago there was a lively spirit, a smile, a sudden laugh, a brightness that said she was alive and happy. Now these had disappeared.

She spoke only broken English despite more than sixty years of living in Canada. I remember now that this never surprised me. Looking back it really is not at all hard to understand.

He is a large burly-faced man, unbent by the years. A muscular barrel chest gives an appearance of unusual strength that is belied by a quick and easy smile. Gnarled hands and thick fingers suggest hard work, yet he was known for the delicate willow baskets he made as a hobby. Indeed he joked that he was called "artiste" by the more pretentious of those who purchased the products of his passing time. Thinning grey hair, thick glasses, and words spoken softly in a hesitant, almost shy, way gave the impression of a gentle old age, of a life calmly winding down. Despite diabetes, atrial fibrillation, and chronic lung disease, he was alive in the important ways. He had hopes and dreams and a desire to live every day.

He had immigrated to Canada from Eastern Europe in 1921. She came a few years later once he was established with work and solid prospects. Their entire lives were spent in the area to which they originally came. Constant change was foreign to them; they needed stability, permanence. They worked hard, in modest jobs, had three sons and a degree of achievement that marked their lives as successful. It should have led to a happy old age; it should have been their time. They deserved rest and peace.

That everyone grows old is no revelation. But to grow old with someone you have spent a lifetime loving may be either great comfort or great tragedy. If nature is kind you may age together in the comedy of dementia or in the wisdom of many years. Yet seldom is the cosmos so benevolent. Too often the roads of our aging are widely divergent. One stays alert and alive; though the heart fails, the kidneys slow, and lungs grow cloudy, some spark, some vitality remains. Within limits medicine can deal with the problems of a failing body. But if one grows old in mind and retreats into a private world of dementia, confusion, and paranoia, then the other is left to suffer for both. Medical hi-tech can deal with an aging body far more efficiently than it can cope with a dying mind.

Such was their tragedy. She became more and more alone, living for ever longer periods apart from everyone but the demons in her mind. At first she was only forgetful; then she became confused, paranoid, and hopelessly senile. And finally she wandered into her own world of long ago and didn't return. She was alive in body and carried on with the mechanics of living, but that part of her which gave her identity, that made her an individual, had vanished. With this, he dealt as long and as well as he could, longer perhaps than most would. He absorbed her accusations and threats though they pained him deeply. He assumed responsibility for their lives. He cooked. He cleaned. He arranged everything and he steadfastly rejected any offer of institutionalizing her. He cared too deeply. The love of so many years could not understand and could not reconcile past and present.

Their house was a modest bungalow in a middle-class subdivision. It looked well cared for, like the symbol of new world affluence that it was. In a quiet neighbourhood where small children played in the streets without fear, it reflected the tranquillity their lives should have had.

The act seemed particularly grizzly: an old lady bludgeoned to death with a hammer; an old man near death with a stab wound to the abdomen. Rumours circulate quickly in a small town. Before long, everyone from a crazed drug dealer to a serial killer had been implicated. The truth was much less complicated. Much sadder.

The phone call to my office was starkly simple. It shattered the calm of a quiet morning office. "Mr. W. is here; he's killed his wife and stabbed himself with a butcher knife." The pain in the ER nurse's voice was as obvious as my silent disbelief.

As I saw him in the Emergency Department he was quite calm. He explained that she was trying to leave the house again, that she would not listen, that the anger he had so long contained could not be denied, that seeing her fall he turned the hammer on himself and being unable to accomplish what he wished, he had stabbed himself with a knife. He regretted only that he had been unsuccessful and that now much ado would be made of his disposition. It was difficult not to agree with him.

There are no easy answers to the questions that inevitably follow such a tragedy. To ask them is to acknowledge grief and human weakness. To have no answers is to find a common comfort.

The motive seemed as simple as the problem was complex. I knew only that for her any pain had long since vanished into an impenetrable shroud of dementia and for him the pain of living had simply become greater than the pain of dying.

A Christmas Gift

Through sense and nonsense, never out nor in;
Free from all meaning, whether good or bad.
And in one word, heroically mad.

– John Dryden

What a strange and frightening world he must inhabit. How sad that his best, and perhaps only, friend is the doctor he sees for twenty or thirty minutes every two weeks. Does he know that he may live a very long time, but his pain will probably never get better? Does he realize how few answers I have?

My thoughts wander in these totally non-clinical directions as I listen to the aimless and convoluted drone of this long-time psychiatric patient. Not old in years, he is ancient in suffering. He is perhaps as close to hopeless as anyone I have seen; not just in a medical sense, but in a deeply personal, seen-it-all, been-through-the-mill, nobody-willing-to-try-anymore way. He is lost and it is unlikely I will help him to be found.

He is labelled a personality disorder. This is convenient. It makes it easier to give up, to accept that perhaps I can do nothing. They never get better, you know.

He used to be institutionalized. He used to see psychiatrists, psychologists, and nurse counsellors at the mental health centre. Now he sees only me. I seem to be at the bottom of the psychiatric totem pole.

Every two weeks he visits. He is thin and forlorn, his hair long, straight, and as black as the leather jacket he wears year round. His unkempt fingernails are worn, bitten to nothing. His always sad eyes are usually puffy from crying or bruised by self-abuse, or being beaten. A map of scars, mostly self-inflicted, is scattered over his too thin arms. Often he has shown me an Exacto knife blade he keeps in his wallet. When the world becomes too much for him, the pain of cutting flesh momentarily diverts that uncontrollable rage, that never-ending confusion that lives within his mind.

They all tried to make him better, but nothing changed. Perhaps I don't try as hard. Am I viewed as an accomplice? I hardly ever do anything more than listen. When he occasionally stops talking or looks for direction, I try to say something a good bartender might consider comforting. But he is usually off again before I get the chance, off on a tangent without noticeably paying much attention to anything I've said.

Yet he is always so profusely thankful for our brief time. I have become a surrogate father figure. Indeed I find the transference in this psychothera-

comfort with these offerings? The small bottle of perfume and the pen I accepted. They seemed innocent and inexpensive enough. The money I insisted he keep. His eyes began to turn away and the smile I had so rarely seen began to fade. Quickly I suggested he give it to the local food bank, that they needed it more than I. He beamed acceptance. The act of giving seemed to be what mattered. It gave him an immediate purpose. Yes, he would go there right now. And just as I sat down, resigned to accept the usual freefall of words, he handed me a Christmas card and left. Though momentarily stunned, I was too busy to argue my good fortune. The card went into my pocket, forgotten.

Much later, when the cavalcade of the day was over, I reached for something else and found the card and the letter it contained. My Christmas season began as I read on.

"Thank you for taking time to listen to my problems ... for trying to help me. How do I help myself? I'm trying to be strong and unafraid. I want help. You try so hard to tell me I'm somebody and say that I can overcome obstacles and be okay. Thank you for caring. I wish I could tell you everything I have learned. Merry Christmas."

Taped to the inside of the card, with an old bloodstained Band-Aid, was an Exacto knife blade.

I had been given a gift, from the poorest of my poor. I smiled and began to feel less tired, the day seemed less dreary, and my burdens seemed lighter. Perhaps there is hope ... for us all.

An Emergency Room Visit

I had seen birth and death, but had thought
they were different.

– T. S. Eliot

I wonder if all small towns have a police car parked
at the only downtown stoplight at four a.m. It
seems to be there every time I navigate these tired
streets so late. Always unoccupied, it provides just
enough intimidation to make me wait for the light to
change before broaching the intersection. Sometimes
in a flash of defiance I violate the red light, inviting,
even welcoming, the sirens that never follow. If they
dared, my righteous indignation would overflow. A
knight on a sacred crusade could be no more filled
with false moral superiority.

It is early spring and the night is unseasonably
warm, even soft, like emotional velvet. The streets
are empty, as asleep as I wish that I were. My original almost anger at this intrusion into my dreams
has given way to an "it goes with the territory" res-

ignation, an acceptance. Yet I think the anger never entirely disappears.

Sometimes these middle of the night calls to come to the Emergency Room seem to reflect all the injustices I've ever suffered. A self-pitying "Why me?" screams silently in my mind. Once again I've forgotten to turn down the volume on the bedside phone. When it rings, I awaken like a runner to a starter's pistol. The adrenalin is immediately there anticipating direction. But often it has nowhere to go.

Tonight is such an occasion. An eighty-year-old diabetic, post CVA (Cerebral Vascular Accident), in acute congestive heart failure has arrived in the ER via ambulance with family in tow. Could I please come now? Having heard the story from the ER nurse my mind slows down, but it's too late. The bounding pulse and that unseen angst that accompany an adrenalin rush persist. They must burn themselves out in the fullness of their brief time. No more sleep tonight.

It's only a short drive to the hospital, less than five minutes really. At this hour, the dark, the quiet, the fatigue, seem to eliminate so much of the chaff that so often clogs my mind. Suddenly, complex problems become simple, solutions obvious, issues clear.

My mind wanders to the metaphysical. Is there much thought that precedes dying? Or is death an automatic function requiring no voluntary attention, no conscious action? It dawns on me. This lady has come to make one last effort at living and I'm going to formalize the attempt.

My thoughts grow more cosmic. I recognize that I've seen both ends of some immense spectrum. Life begins and life ends. And in between we do the best we can. No prizes. No punishment. Just living.

Far enough, some barely conscious sensibility cries. I surface now and realize that my thoughts have all the practical implications of Kant's categorical imperative. All this in the five-minute drive to the hospital.

My car seems to guide itself into the empty parking lot. I'm preoccupied with wondering if all small community hospitals have excellent nursing staff simply because they are often the only ones around. They become less dependent when there's no one to slough all problems unto. As I enter the Emergency Department all is well in hand. An IV is running TKO (to keep [the vein] open) and an oxygen mask is comforting. A family crowds anxiously around the stretcher, whispering. I wonder why they are whispering. My examination only verifies the obvious.

Mrs. M is old and tired, and too short of breath to have much interest in living. Her heart is fibrillating, her lungs are labouring, her kidneys have stopped working, and her mind is content to concentrate on dying. All else becomes superfluous.

A daughter with whom she lives urges, "Let her go." A son rushes in from the evening rain shouting loudly and authoritatively, "It's not her time." I wonder what Mrs. M feels. But she's unable to say, and I can only guess.

She survives the Emergency Room and her condition stabilizes on the brink. The ICU (Intensive

Care Unit) and Step-down units are not interested, so she goes to a medical floor. In the morning one of my colleagues will continue to urge life from a body seeking death. The battle will rage for a few days. Then he will lose. Has she won? Was she even playing the game?

I drive home more slowly than I came, enjoying the stillness of the night. Enjoying, too, the waning adrenalin and the clarity, even simplicity, with which the world is now presenting itself.

Sleep ... no more. It is after five a.m. I stop at the local Tim's for a doughnut and coffee. Now I know where the occupant of the deserted police car is. I can't help a small laugh. This only draws a curious glance from a tired salesgirl.

Watching the sunrise from my deck will be pleasant this morning. Perhaps more revelations are yet to come.

Later today I'll regret my lack of sleep, but now it seems almost a reward, a gate to some inner tranquillity. I've almost forgiven fate for dragging me away in the first place.

In a few hours the world will be new again. Endless cycles will begin as they have every day since a time long forgotten. In the office I will see the sick, the near sick, and those to whom sickness is a stranger. I will try to be patient and understand them all as best I can. Perhaps I'll even try a little harder today, because at four o'clock this morning it seemed so clear. Life begins, life ends, and in between you do the best you can.

Death and Courage

Any man's death diminishes me,
because I am involved in mankind;
and therefore never send to know for whom
the bell tolls;
it tolls for thee.

– John Donne

She is thirty-eight years old. She is dying. Some-time in the next few weeks I will drive out to her home in the country and pronounce her dead. I will mumble platitudes. I will say that large doses of morphine kept her comfortable. I will not add, as comfortable as you can be when you are dying of widespread metastasis from a malignant lung tumour. I will say she died peacefully.

If it is late evening or early morning, I will wonder if her husband is going to wake their children to tell them that their mother is dead. Or will he let them sleep until the sun rises? Is death easier to explain under the light of a blue sky? After all, it is expected and what could they do anyway? A few less hours of sadness might be worth the wait.

I had nothing to offer when the diagnosis was made. A referral back to the cancer clinic was the best I could do. I have nothing but words now. I will speak in a hushed voice, in clichés and euphemisms: no more pain, gone to a better place. But I cannot begin to understand the agony of her death, nor its impact, nor any higher purpose for it. The best I can manage is a grudging acceptance that is more resignation than insight.

Barely six months from the time of diagnosis she dies. I am filled with a vague uneasiness as I drive to the house. There are so many cars in the laneway that I can scarcely find room. The family has gathered and prays the rosary; tears have come and gone. Her husband and children are subdued, serious, but remarkably calm, almost serene.

I am led to a small alcove, a makeshift bedroom on the ground floor. A single bed fills the middle of a room bathed in morning sunlight. Her frail figure, clothed in a nightgown and warmly covered with a duvet, rests there. Pictures, mementoes, reminders of life, are all around the bed, making this last sanctum almost joyous.

To pronounce someone dead seems more the domain of a priest than a physician. I dutifully confirm the obvious and after quiet words and a few handshakes I leave discreetly, feeling an irrational sense of failure and guilt. Could I have done more?

F.T. is thirty-five years old. He used to manage a small business. He has had a malignant brain tumour for three years. A recent CT scan showed a shrinking, almost disappearance, of the oligodendro-cytoma that the neurosurgeon was unable to wholly excise. The "almost" will kill him someday soon.

He asks me what he should do. He feels well. He feels normal ... now. Neither I nor the consultants are willing to place any remotely precise time frame on his life. I offer him statistics. He continues to wonder. Should he run as fast as he can through what remains of his life, or should he withdraw and quietly prepare; summarize his life and simply wait? These questions overwhelm me. They seem too personal. I feel privileged and uncomfortable in the same instant.

He chooses to live until he dies. He studies to become an accountant. His courage astounds me. The course of study is longer than the statistics would allow him.

I cannot pretend to understand why he is still alive. I can only accept his life with the same strained equanimity with which I have accepted the deaths of others.

It's four a.m. I have just returned from watching K.R. die. She was fifty-nine. Her husband told me this evening that they would have been married forty years tomorrow had not colon cancer intervened. He held her hand as she gradually stopped breathing. Not many hours earlier she had weakly acknowledged my presence with her eyes and a few unintelligible words.

What went on behind those eyes? I comfort myself by reasoning that she was too far along to be aware of very much. But how can I know what ease or what anguish or even what comfort carried her away? I close her eyes in the manner of old movies and give him a prescription for Ativan. The funeral home is called; the paperwork arranged. A brief handshake, a few empty and generic words, and I steal away into the morning darkness.

A.N. was fifty-two when he died. There was no warning. He simply died, quietly, quickly, cleanly, while he slept. He leaves a wife and four children. He had lived a blue-collar life in a small town: straightforward, honest, unpretentious, and essentially good. His death, like his life, seemed to lack any melodrama. It, too, was straightforward, honest, and unpretentious.

He coached his son's hockey team. Our kids were the same age and often played together. He was always pleasant, always kind, always supportive of and encouraging to the kids. I never heard him speak ill of anyone. He was without guile or malice. I wept for this good man.

Death comes easily and often into my world. One lives, another dies, without rhyme or reason. It's part of the territory, I guess. For the most part it remains clinical, emotionally distant. I may analyze but I cannot agonize. I cannot. That price is too high. Yet I always feel less human if I am not touched by its sting. I regret profoundly their passing. I mourn for their families. I miss their presence. I don't pretend to understand the larger why of their deaths.

Perhaps in them I have seen myself or at least that part of myself which is most human. I have seen all the potential of life in death. I have seen courage and fear, hope in the face of endless pain, and acceptance after hope dies. I have seen the essence of living fulfilled and transcended in an instant. I have seen the face of God. Where can I possibly go from here?

My Son

To make your children capable of honesty is the beginning of education.

– John Ruskin

It must be two in the morning. Without a clock I'm not terribly sure, though. I don't like clocks. Just something else telling you what to do. Anyway, it's late, really late.

The old black phone beside my parents' bed is making that awful sound. Dad picks it up. With a few grunts, a sigh, and maybe a few choice words, he realizes he must go and struggles slowly out of bed. The clothes he took off a few hours earlier are on again. From my upstairs room I see the car move slowly out of the driveway and make its way toward the hospital.

I don't know what he did during those late-night visits. My interest only went as far as the end of the driveway before sleep reclaimed me. By the next morning I would have forgotten the intrusion, although Dad still may not have been home. Or if he was he may have been quieter and looked more tired. From time to time, usually when I was younger, I would ask why he went or who got hurt. I understand more now and don't ask as much. Most often I would get a flip response, a light-hearted dismissal of any middle of the night problems. Sometimes there was only silence. Often a tangent would follow. Glancing up from his morning sports' section, he might offer a challenge that Larry Bird was the most rounded basketball player of all time or that any of the original six would cake-walk to the Stanley Cup today.

Some nights I awoke at two a.m. even though the phone didn't ring. These nights he slept undisturbed. I alone awoke.

Dad could not completely separate his family from his work. When I was younger, too young to understand much beyond the difference between presence and absence, I accompanied him to the hospital, usually for rounds on the weekend. I suppose it made me feel pretty important. After all, he was my dad and he was a doctor.

The nurses would comment on how I had his eyes and how we had the same slow shuffling walk, head down and hands thrust deeply into pockets. Blushing, I would protest that we were really quite different ... all the while hoping that their words were true.

I would wait outside a patient's room or at the nursing station. Occasionally I was invited in by my dad or the patient. It is after all a small hospital in a small town. Everyone knows everyone else. Patients were often friends as well.

Maybe my most fond memories of these hospital visits are the mad races we used to have down the stairs. Four flights of stairs in less than fifteen seconds. I always seemed to win. As much as I wanted to take the elevator, Dad would insist we couldn't wait and the dash for the next floor would begin. Luckily, we were in a hospital in case of an injury, but I cannot recall any such occurrence. I don't think he raced at two in the morning.

The perspective of time allows me to say that Dad wasn't around as much as he might have liked in my early years. He often worked in the ER or delivered babies or did anaesthesia. These activities and the meetings he dreaded seemed to begin when regular office hours ended. Sometimes I rarely saw him for days.

Yet when he was home he tried to make the best of it. However tired or distracted, he would catch my wild pitches, play one on one, help me to add, or teach me to read. He refused as best he could to let being a doctor totally disrupt his family or at least disrupt it past a certain point.

It would be a lie to say his absences had no effect. I grew closer to my mother; she was always there. At eight years old it is a lot easier to love someone who is around most of the time. I wasn't always sure what he was doing, but I knew it wasn't with me. At two in the morning he might have come up to give me a kiss, but I was already sleeping.

53

I wonder if the key to understanding my dad as a father and a doctor is to look into his father's eyes. They are soft eyes on a hard face wrinkled with age and hard work. My grandfather was for many years a farmer and worked long hours to send three children through university. All graduated, several times, and became successful in their separate fields.

Once at the dining room table of a family gathering, my sister, soon to enter her first year of university, spoke of the unfair treatment of those who were denied student loans because of perceived parental ability to pay. My grandfather listened not so patiently and while peering down the table at her, he spoke in this thick German-Hungarian accent. Although I can't remember the exact words, it was something about a family to be raised, fed, clothed, sheltered, and sent through school entirely on the sweat of his brow. He seemed outraged by the sentiment of being able to get something worthwhile without working hard for it. At two in the morning he was often in the fields or kilns checking on his tobacco crop, simply because it needed to be done.

As I have gotten older I recognize a few more lines on my dad's face. He speaks to me more often now about what he does. What strikes me most is the ease with which he tells his stories. I remember one about a car accident scene he attended. A head-on collision on a desperately foggy night had left one dead and two seriously injured. Dad recounted briefly how two brothers in one car tried to pass another car. One brother now lay dead in the driver's seat while the other wandered about the scene confused and agitated. His confusion and anxiety, Dad said, were signs of a serious head injury. He later died in hospital. A third victim was trapped in a van into which Dad crawled and started an IV while police, firemen, and ambulance personnel worked to extract this victim. He lived. Later he sent Dad a thank you card. It didn't seem a fair trade.

Such tragedy. Such sadness. How does anyone live with this day after day? He doesn't show much emotion in the telling, only occasionally a kind of resignation or acceptance. His stories are bewildering, haunting. At two in the morning they sometimes come to me. Now I understand the wrinkles and the tired eyes.

* * *

My son is eighteen now. He was younger when he wrote these words. I am not sure why he wrote them or why he gave them to me. I am grateful that he did.

Perhaps putting words on paper is easier than arranging words into sentences spoken out loud. Communication for any adolescent, particularly with a parent, can be a terribly difficult undertaking and comes with all the ease of a comedian struggling to find a lost punchline. Was he trying to tell me something I needed to hear when I had neither the time nor the inclination to listen? Could I have been so deaf all those many years?

I used to think that I was alone, that I worked in isolation. I used to think that only my patients' lives were affected by decisions I made. It gives me pause to read his words. I am relieved that I am not alone. I am saddened that what I do may hurt those I love.

Medicine can be so all consuming. I am too often lost in its vastness, its encompassing effect. Too easily it creeps into every corner of time that I have available. Insidiously it inserts itself into my thoughts. Why do I sometimes keep pen and paper at my bedside and awaken to write down things I must do or have forgotten to do?

We all identify with what we do. It becomes a large part of any definition of ourselves. Sometimes it becomes an obsession. No profession is so large and no person so small as to be enveloped by what they do, even if it is a labour of love.

There must be life beyond medicine, separate physically, separate emotionally. I struggle daily to find the balance. I regret that my son had to show me the way. I weep for time lost and things that cannot be changed. Regret is such an empty emotion. Devoid of value and reeking of self-pity, it's rarely worth the effort. So I'll try to learn. Out of the mouths of babes.

The House Call

Those who love deeply never grow old.

— Dorothy Canfield Fisher

No greater love than this. He was ninety-four. She was eighty-eight. They had been together more than seventy years.

Standing in the doorway of the bedroom, I was hesitant to enter, afraid to intrude. A very old man lay uncovered, almost naked, and motionless on a large double bed. An old woman patiently changed his diaper and cleaned his incontinence from an ugly sacral ulcer. She spoke quiet, comforting words that came easily, for her frail partner of so many years.

Is he still alive? I wondered. Can he hear or feel this gentle ministering? I know that her soft touch and kind words have done more to keep him alive than all of my medicines.

I entered quietly and asked after him. "It's not been a good day," was all that she replied. She looked tired, sad in a resigned, accepting sort of way. I wonder if there is a special weariness that accompanies caring for a dying lover.

I moved around the bed to face him and took his hand, squeezing it lightly in greeting. He opened his eyes and raised them toward me. There was a brief smile of recognition, but no words followed before the eyes closed again. The time for words was past.

My examination revealed only the obvious: a rapid irregular pulse, short laboured breaths, and a blood pressure too low. I knew I was seeing a man at the natural end of his life. I felt more a sense of wonder and privilege than of sadness. It seemed easy to wax philosophic when there was nothing left to do.

How facile my council and gentle pat on his arm. "Rest now," I said. The final rest would come soon enough, I thought. A silent prayer for the dying followed and I wondered if this was not the most useful thing that I did. The limitations of my medicine never seemed as obvious and necessary. I felt relieved that I could not and perhaps should not do anything more.

I asked if I might speak to her. We sat quietly at the kitchen table and talked about a "Do Not Resuscitate" order. Just how much did she wish me to do? What was I capable of doing? The enormity of this conversation did not dawn on me until later. She was being asked to decide what efforts would be made to keep him alive. Her whole life had been directed at living and here in an instant I wanted her to change that focus, to decide how death might come more easily. How could I suggest that, or offer to remove him from his home to die among strangers, in a place he did not know? Her wisdom and serenity shamed my uncertainty. He would die as he had lived, quietly, simply, with his family, in his home.

My insecurity surfaced. I changed his medication a bit. I thought this might make him more comfortable, but perhaps it was for my sake more than his; perhaps I did need to assure myself that I was doing something. More's the pity. Nothing was what screamed to be done.

I let myself quietly out the unlocked front door, suspecting that I would be back soon. And she returned to her vigil at the bedside. I had no doubt she would still be there when I came again.

My drive home was silent, pensive. Confessing to myself an admiration for the calm dignity with which they had chosen to approach death, I simply didn't know if I had that kind of courage. That night I sat quietly with my wife Clare, watching but not seeing the TV, and I asked her if she would change my diaper when I was ninety-four. At first she laughed and joked that I was on my own. When she realized I was serious, she softly replied that yes, she thought she would. This unhappy image becomes a source of joy to me. I find comfort in the simple devotion, the caring that it implies. Am I capable of such love? Am I deserving of such love? Are any of us?

I returned a day or two later. The scene had changed little. More family – children, grandchildren, and great-grandchildren – were gathered. His place and hers remained the same.

My presence seemed an unnecessary formality.

I had only to confirm the obvious and sign a few papers. A priest had been called and had come before me. The order of things was correctly established.

She was not crying. Relieved or apart seemed a more appropriate description. It wasn't until later, when she became ill, that fully I understood. She was just putting in time now. I had been witness to the final chapter in a profoundly human love story. Amidst all the sorrow I became envious.

A Very Human Parade

*Remember, Man; Thou art dust and unto dust
thou shalt return.*

– Genesis 3:19

Patients are intriguing people. They come in all sizes, shapes, colours, and ages. And they carry with them the most interesting lives. The baggage they bring is sometimes dragged along like an unwanted guest and sometimes it's a picnic basket on a pleasant walk.

Daily I watch a human parade. I see some winners and some losers, but mostly I see the contenders, those who try so hard every day with measures of both success and failure. And still they go on. Medication, monitoring, and the concerns of a fellow traveller are my tools. Rarely can I offer absolute cures and even more rarely do I have nothing to give. I welcome them in and bid them adieu: delivery and dispatch. And in between I am granted the privilege of access to their most hidden secrets, their joys and sorrows, and that complex medley of experiences that make up their lives. I take far more than I give. They become a sort of library of life where I can learn so much.

Miss C never married. I remember she told me once of a wartime romance that ended sadly when he didn't return. After that nothing ever happened. Never mind, she would say, her life was full of so many other things. She's almost 101 years old now. I contemplate all those years and everything they imply: the changes she has seen, the wisdom that so many years must impart. She's blind now, but she has adapted as well as anyone can. Perhaps over the years she has seen enough to last a lifetime. But this is a pretentious judgement on my part. I remind myself to observe and not to assume. At my last visit she told me that she is ready to die and wondered why she is still alive. I thought the question was rhetorical and remained silent. She laughed.

Miss C has no immediate family. Yet she seems happy enough. Perhaps the drive to immortalize ourselves in our children is not as strong or necessary as I thought. I see her only rarely now. She lives in a retirement home and I visit less often than she wishes. In this way I am less apt to do something medically appropriate, but quite unnecessary. Good luck, genetics, and some higher power have contributed more to her longevity than I ever have. Her body is dwindling now. She is small and stooped under the weight of so many years. Her senses seem to be retreating. Eyesight gone, hearing reduced. Osteoarthritis and a hip fracture two years ago have limited her mobility. Her heart beats irregularly and her kidneys function only poorly. Physically she has returned to the basics: eat, sleep, eliminate.

It's odd how her mind has not aged. Even as her body has moved from infancy to maturity to the infancy of old age, she remains bright, alert, and alive. She laughs often and doesn't dwell on the sorrows or triumphs of the past unless asked. I think she continues to grow and isn't getting older at all. She is all the ages she ever was, and she revels in each and every one. She is a living celebration.

When does the mind die? Or is it simply released from a body to continue growing elsewhere? Maybe that's what a soul is.

If I only sit and listen, Miss C teaches so much. She accepts her life for what it has been, is now, and will be tomorrow. She seems above most worldly cares. If she lives another day so be it. If she doesn't, I suspect that this wouldn't really trouble her very much. But perhaps I am assuming again. I envy her peace. Let the future bring what it may, she will be ready.

Multiple sclerosis is such a tragic disease. It has robbed M of a life, her children of a mother, and her mother of a daughter. She has lived on the chronic care floor of the hospital now for several years and no longer speaks or has any independence. She is barely middle-aged. Her husband died suddenly of a heart attack a few months ago. He used to take her home on weekends to spend time with family. This was a monumental undertaking. I admired his courage. The family decided not to tell her. They thought, they hoped, she was too far gone to know the difference. They wanted to spare her the pain. She used to recognize her husband sometimes. But mostly, she didn't. Yet she called me by his name one day when I was making rounds. Even though she seems indifferent to most things now, I think she knows and wonders why he no longer visits.

She may live a long time yet, but I don't think she will. She has begun to fail. Not eating. Swallowing with more difficulty. Less responsive than usual. She seems sad at times, although it's difficult to tell from the outside. I think she knows that time is short. Sometimes I wonder what goes on beneath that dense veil of chronic illness that now shrouds her life. I hope she has not become her disease and that something of her remains. I think I see it occasionally in her unexpected smile. But maybe this is just what I want to see.

I can know so little about her. Is she anxious to move on? Is she tired? Does she still ask why? Of whom? Does she still have the courage to believe in God? In herself? In anything? I can't begin to know, but I think she does.

I am saddened by all the loss and pain she and her family have experienced. I am strangely happy that I can feel this sadness. From them I have learned about faith, acceptance, courage, and pain without words.

Mr. J could speak no more than a little English despite decades of living in Canada. But his halting and unsure speech always came with a quick smile and an easy laugh. When he first visited me, he was already in his late seventies, but was still a large, robust man. Ever the old-world gentleman, he would extend his hand in greeting and rise from his chair as I entered the examining room. We spoke sometimes about his frequent trips to his lush green island homeland. His was the stereotypical old-world-to-new, rags-to-riches life.

How hard it was to tell him he was dying. Cancer of the prostate, widespread metastasis, surgery, chemotherapy, palliation. The grim cascade reminds me of how little I can do.

Mercifully, he died quietly and quickly, in his home, in his bed, surrounded by his wife and children. I wonder if this made a difference to him. I hope it did. I hope it brought some comfort to his family. He struggled only briefly to keep living. I think this is a reflex we all have even when we wait to die. I will remember him fondly.

Ms. T was a business manager. She has lost this and almost everything else. She used to be called manic depressive but now her pigeonhole is bipolar disorder, type one. It hasn't made any difference. If she had any insight she would see her life spiralling ever downward. She doesn't. Perhaps that's for the best. I'm not sure it would matter. Knowing what lies ahead and being incapable of doing much about it might be even more depressing.

I wonder about her future. Will she ever get better, even a little? Will she live to experience crisis as a special event rather than a way of life? Will she ever live unsupported by the latest pharmaceutical miracles? I don't think so. Her mental illness is deeply ingrained. Without it there would be a void. I think she's already lost sight of who she once was. I struggle not to. Perhaps if I can keep what she used to be in sight, hope will remain. At least in my eyes.

Every day they bring me their pain. It becomes an offering, a challenge. That I feel its sting reminds me of our shared humanity. Even when I cannot change an outcome, this sharing enables me to listen with a little more concern, if only perhaps because I see myself. I see all of us in their broken hearts and lost dreams, their struggles and sorrows, their joy in living and their sadness in dying. I have seen a common humanity. What a grand and glorious journey it has been. And what a wonderful perspective from which to watch a parade.

Babies

And she who gives a baby birth
Brings saviour Christ again to earth

– John Masefield

It's late again. Very late. I'm tired. Later today I'll wish that I had more energy. But wishing doesn't seem to work anymore. There have been too many late nights. While my mind forgives, my body demands recovery time I rarely seem to have. Middle-of-the-night obstetrics never gets any easier.

I remember that first delivery. As a medical student I was far removed, standing in an overhead gallery. I was a distant spectator to a small drama. How quiet the delivery room was: epidural quiet, almost serene. Voices were kept low and silence lingered between contractions. The glare of metal and bright lights seemed strangely out of place. The obstetrician sat quietly, fully gowned and waiting with the patience of one who has been this way many times before. Expectation hung in the air like an un-fulfilled promise until a blue-pink squealing baby appeared and changed everything. The facade was shattered. Voices began to carry a certain lilt, almost a song, and smiles stopping just short of laughter appeared on everyone. A sense of joy seemed to pre-vail. I remember a kind of wonder, an amazement, at the transformations and the complex simplicity of the whole process.

And now, many hundred deliveries later, I re-main a wonderstruck spectator. Obstetrics seems an area of medicine less touched by that cynicism born of experience. It is by and large a happy event attended by healthy people. It is that rare area of medicine that does not, usually, deal with illness or sadness.

It's strange how memories build up over the years. Whether we want them or not, they accumu-late like old books we can't throw away but only occasionally take the time to open. They are good and bad, comfortable and threatening, welcome friends and uninvited guests.

I remember the socio-intellectually-emotionally deprived fifteen- and sixteen-year-olds who couldn't get by the Barbie doll concept of babies; their pain punctuated by screams; their child-like joy marked by giggles. The infant struggles to be born, is briefly fondled, loved as a child would love a new toy, and ignored when playtime becomes troublesome, and reality interferes. Lasting love might be a stranger to this child. But I am also amazed at the capacity of a baby to mature an adult, to inspire growth and love.

I remember thinking that there was always joy in the delivery room, excepting for those moments of congenital or man-made tragedy. But the real world has taught me that the birth of a child is not always cause for celebration.

I remember the Mexican Mennonite ladies whose charts say twenty-five, but whose faces say forty, whose bodies were tired of almost yearly pregnancies and whose affect was flattened by the thought of yet another mouth to feed on labourer's wages. There seemed little room for joy.

And I remember Mrs. P whom I thought would be such a case. She was thirty-three years old, but looked older and acted wiser. Her antenatal care had been minimal. Much of her pregnancy had been spent in Mexico with her family of seasonal farm workers. This was to be her eighth child and tenth pregnancy.

As she laboured quietly, I wondered if she noticed the difference between the sanitized hospital setting she was now in and the plainly substandard (in our view) setting of her home deliveries in Mexico. I remember thinking, How happy an event can this be? But there I was again, imposing my values on someone who doesn't live in my world.

Mrs. P's delivery was a very happy occasion. She laughed and made her few hours of labour little more than child's play. I simply watched, a bystander, again content with performing that most difficult of all obstetrical manoeuvres – sitting on my hands and waiting for something perfectly natural to occur. Her delivery was easy. Her son was healthy. She radiated that joy so particular to the delivery room.

Her very first baby could have been given no greater welcome. This child would be loved.

I remember wondering what his life would be like. His childhood would certainly be spartan and strict. Though poor he might be, he would be well behaved, clean, and strangely stoic in a time when children are more apt to be heard than seen. As a teenager he would realize how different he was from his peers. He will probably leave school very early and work at some menial labour. He'll marry young and with his wife will have six, seven, or eight children. His entire life will be spent within the confines of his family, community, and church. It will be no different than his grandfather's was or his children's will be. And will he be less happy? There is something to be said for the security of knowing.

Is it a sign of age that I project a lifetime onto a newborn child, that I try to imagine the future of each one: this one will be happy, this one will have a difficult time, this one begins with advantages, this one has peaked at birth? Is this an unconscious recognition that I won't be around to see it happen, that my life is finite?

I grow old. I grow old. Today I delivered the baby of a mother I delivered many years ago. It didn't dawn on me until afterwards. This was the child of a child I had delivered. Time is unkind to remind me of how quickly the years pass and how little they change.

I remember long hours of obstetrical work and moments of sheer panic: the shoulders that wouldn't deliver, the umbilical cords that came first, the too-late discovered breeches, the uterus that delivered with the placenta, the bleeding that wouldn't stop, the cruel tracing of the foetal monitor telling me something had to be done.

But mostly I remember the good times: the fathers who laughed and cried, the mothers who tried so hard, the uncomplicated start of wonderfully complex lives. I often wondered why they were so profuse with their thank you's, when I usually had done little more than watch, wait, and catch the baby.

I think I'll stop doing obstetrics soon. The medico-legal climate grows more treacherous yearly and the hours wear harder. Yet some part of me will hesitate, anxious to continue as some sort of witness and ever ready to remember.

The Victory of Age

Old age hath yet his honour and his toil.
Death closes all; but something ere the end,
Some work of noble note may yet be done.
                              – Alfred, Lord Tennyson

The house is nondescript – a small bungalow be-hind a large shopping mall. A relatively new exterior is marked by dullness and lack of activity. The grass is always too long and the flowers have long ago given up.

My car is unnoticed as I pull into an empty driveway. A thinly disguised commotion is settling as I enter. Usually I don't knock. At first I felt something of an intruder walking in so unannounced. But this has faded, much like the guilt I experienced when first working with quadriplegics. Reality intervenes. Rose is ninety-five years old and quite deaf. She rarely knows I'm there until I stand beside her and shout into her ear.

Occasionally I'm greeted by one of the several social agencies that visit regularly, or by one of her intellectually disabled daughters, each past sixty and living in a child's world of long ago. Whatever will become of them when Rose is gone? Although she hasn't told me so, I suspect thoughts of this trouble Rose greatly.

Inside, the house smells of age and disability unable to fully cope with daily living; of bodies and clothes too long unwashed and of services that come not often enough. Colours are faded and furniture is outdated and worn.

The walls are adorned with grey-black photos of generations long past, fine mustachioed, unsmiling men and solemn be-frocked women; people and places that only Rose can identify. Interspersed are colour Polaroids of rosy-cheeked great-grandchildren whose names she can't remember. Framed letters display congratulations from premiers and a prime minister. Growing old is perhaps an achievement of sorts, although Rose has never mentioned this.

She sits in her favourite chair beside a large picture window in a living room cluttered with the bric-a-brac of a lifetime. A walker remains directly before her, an arm's reach away. Her eyesight is almost as bad as her hearing. I remind myself that sunlight can be felt as well as seen.

On a small stand to her right sits a collection of pills, the magic she believes is keeping her alive: Lasix, Lanoxin, blood pressure pills, some vitamins, assorted eye drops, and a cream or two.

Rose. So frail. So strong. Thin, wispy grey hair, sallow skin that sags from her face and limbs, eyes that radiate more light than her clouded corneas can admit. I remember my surprise when she survived and returned home after a fractured hip three years ago. The body wears down, but the mind remains alert, the spirit burns on, and the soul glows brilliantly.

She is the inspiration that binds this family together and keeps it functioning. Was it courage that helped her raise her handicapped children without institutional help ... or was it necessity ... or was it love? I suspect it's all of these. I also suspect it doesn't matter and that she hasn't given it much thought. It was done simply because they were hers. Parenting at its finest.

Rose's faith in medicine is perhaps greater than mine. I visit her less often than she wishes. She interprets this as small-town too busy. I tend to believe that this way I'll have less chance of inflicting some unneeded medical intervention when I don't know what else to do. I've come to realize that Rose's genes and some measure of good luck are probably more responsible for her ninety-five years than medicine ever could be. My services here are, perhaps, more apt to produce harm than good.

We talk. Rather, I shout and Rose responds to questions never asked. Her smile and lively wit communicate more about her health than my stethoscope. She scolds me for being so long in coming. I feign remorse. She is concerned that her daughter Ruth doesn't want to go to school anymore. Should she be allowed to stay home? I suppress a smile. At age sixty-five I guess Ruth could perhaps stay home. And yes, it would be fine to take an extra vitamin E capsule every day. Indeed, Rose, you are looking remarkably well. Your blood pressure is good and I'm pleased there is less swelling in your legs today.

This is totally banal banter, but so necessary. The real communication lies between the words. Like so many disguises they mask the intent of our exchange. Rose cannot say, "I'm old. I've lived long and well. Comfort me, and help me to go 'gently into my good night.'" And I cannot say, "Rose, tell me your secrets, your wisdom of so many years."

I stop wondering why I've come this time. It strikes me somewhat suddenly. I've come to marvel at the human condition glorified in this frail body almost devoid of senses. Rose is a survivor, but more than that, a survivor of ninety-five hard years, of a lifetime of trials. Yet she is a survivor of wit and joy. Not hers is the bitter cynicism of the defeated. She exudes the nobility of being alive and enjoying it when there doesn't appear to be any reason she should be either. I sense hope for us all in the smile of this one tired old lady.

I leave a little more refreshed than when I came, more hopeful about the day ahead. I think I'll return a bit sooner next time.

Thank You

At times our own light goes out and is rekindled by a spark from another person. Each of us has cause to think with deep gratitude of those who have lit the flame within us.

– Albert Schweitzer

I am sometimes quietly moved by my patients. By what they say or how they act. By how they live or sometimes how they die. To have opportunity to learn from this unique interaction of physician and patient is surely among those intangible rewards that medical practice brings. But I mean learning beyond the clinical facts. I mean a learning that makes you not necessarily a better doctor, but a more human individual.

It is from people such as these that I have learned much. H.M. is a frightened, confused, lonely old lady. She is not alone, nor afraid of being alone. Her loneliness exists in a longing for times past, for the man who was with her for more than sixty years, and for the life they had. Her confusion is in not understanding where or why that has gone and her fright comes from all the unknown fears and doubts that precede dying.

I long to comfort her, to tell her that the end of living is as natural as the beginning, that fear is all right and can be dealt with. Instead, I report that her blood pressure and heart seem good and her sugar is not too high today. She leaves feeling she has the mechanics to carry on for another month. I wonder why she is concerned with doing so and why I haven't been able to make her feel a bit more able to deal with her life.

When she dies, I won't be able to stop myself feeling a sad happiness that she no longer has to play at being alive when her interest has long since vanished.

C.C. is a seventeen-year-old child going on twelve, trying to act twenty-five. She succeeds only at twelve. She lives at home with her poor, middle-aged parents and elderly grandparents and she sleeps in one bed with her two younger sisters. She has been out of grade nine only long enough to become pregnant. In a few months, she will give birth to a baby that she wishes to keep. Being born may be the high point of this child's life.

In labour, her seventeen-year-old body will scream with the pain a twelve-year-old mind cannot understand. Afterward, she will hold the baby as a symbol that she has succeeded in becoming a woman. She is trapped in a life over which she has only periodic control. It is the only symbol she has.

I long to tell her that dice cast at age seventeen don't end your life – that there is so much more to experience, things at which she has never had a chance; that there are oceans to cross, books to read and so many, many things to learn.

But her child/woman's eyes would dull and she would think me crazy. So I tell her the baby is fine and all will be well. I arrange her mother's allowance and feel more than a little hypocritical.

W.Z. died at age fifty-eight. He never understood why. He never asked. His teeth were terribly bad and he wanted them pulled. This was the only comfort I could offer before he became comatose. I wonder if his pain was eased by this simple act and whether it became a cry of victory over the cancer he never faced.

Courage is something most of us don't deal with very much. Our lives are too plain, too safe and controlled for it to be necessary. However, I am happily moved when I can still recognize heroism in the manner in which some people live and die.

A.M. showed such courage. As he lay dying he wondered whether his nine-year-old daughter was at "too tender an age" to accept his death. His other children, somewhat older, were well prepared. His life was in order. As the brain tumour grew, he lost neither his love for life nor his humour and control. I knew him as a teacher and felt very much the proselyte as he spoke of dying. He remained alive in all the most important ways until the moment of the death he so calmly went toward. I pray God grant me that same courage and, even more, the ability to help others achieve it.

Pain is often more than physical discomfort. It is a reflection of lives lost through neglect. When generation after generation lives with broken dreams or false hopes, and promises unfulfilled, the product is predictable.

R.B. is angry and poor. He has pain that no one can cure and, what's worse, no one can even tell him why he has it. So he is angry at everyone, including himself. An all-enveloping bitterness fills him. He has not the insight to accept or understand his life. He is sure he has been cheated. I wish I could reach him. I wish I could help him. Even though I have no answers, I try to offer sympathy and understanding. But the chasm is too great. He moves from consultant to consultant, from shaman to charlatan, in endless pursuit of answers to which there are no questions.

Perhaps happiness lies in the simplicity not to ask complicated questions, but merely to live; to see that those things we too often consider important are really not that consequential, and that real joy must lie in the journey of every day.

G.L. exudes an almost palpable joy as she delivers her second child. She laughs and cries all in the same breath. All pain is forgotten. This is the child of a second marriage and a life reclaimed at an age when she might have given it up for lost. She is a triumph of the will to succeed in being happy. I am grateful for the opportunity to participate in this victory.

Over the years, I have taken so much more than I have given. Those who have passed so transiently through my life have left an indelible impression as they have walked in and out of my door. I have learned so much from their brief passages. When I stop this learning, I probably need to stop practising medicine.

To all of them – the good, the bad, the indifferent, the all-knowing, the tragic, the pathetic, and, most of all, the happy – thank you.

The Existentialism of Birds

Life is an illness to which sleep provides relief
every sixteen hours.
It's a palliative. The remedy is death.

– Nicolas Chamfort

I wonder if birds are aware of death. They will begin singing at about five o'clock this morning.
Would they whistle more quietly, more sombrely if
they knew? Or perhaps they simply don't care. More
likely they recognize the end to be as ordinary and
meaningless as the beginning; like the songs they
sing, a necessary consequence of being alive. Maybe
instinct makes acceptance easier. Existentialism is
easy when you're a bird.

Thoughts seem to wander into my mind, stay a
while, and then leave without much opposition, ap-
proval, or censure of any kind. I've become detached
from them, content only to observe.

It's now three a.m. on a soft spring evening.
I'm tired. The dashboard lights provide only an

eerie illumination in this moonless black and quiet night. I prefer their silence and the entertainment in my head to the chatter of the untouched radio. The headlights seem to lead me along the empty highway. They will guide me to an isolated farmhouse in the country. It's not far really, only twenty or thirty minutes out of town on the road to the lake.

Her daughter didn't sound overly upset on the phone. It just needed to be done so that the funeral home could come and get her. Would I come now and do whatever it is I do and sign the papers?

A tired old farm dog languished on the porch, barely raised its head and didn't bark at all as I entered the laneway. The stillness remained complete. Bare and worn linoleum floors, paint peeling from walls, and shadowy light emanating from a few bare bulbs led me to a room not much bigger than a closet. Lying peacefully on the bed was the object of my early morning wandering.

She had died in her sleep when she was ninety-three years old. She was small, frail, almost wizened, and rigor mortis had already set in. I remember Vince Hanlon's poem: "When I am called in the early morning hours / to declare a dead patient dead / I take two steps into the room / I look at the face of death / and I know deep in my non-medical bowels / that here is a dead man." There is no mystery.

I feel like I should be a priest and perform some ritual. *In nomine patris*, you are now officially dead. Would this be sacrilegious? But all I do is pull the covers up over her head. And this I learned from the movies, not in medical school. I feel a failure.

An elderly daughter wears a look of sad resignation, perhaps having seen her own mortality in the dead eyes of her mother. Tears are absent. She accepts quiet condolences and softly spoken words. My duties end on the telephone, with the funeral director's brusque "Okay, we'll get you to sign it in the morning." An association with a human being whom I had known for many years is thus concluded.

The drive home in the early morning darkness is serene. Catholic habits die hard. I say a silent prayer for the soul newly departed. Science has not yet killed faith. Indeed, as the years go by, I find more comfort in the hope of the latter than in the facts of the former.

My thoughts wander again. Delivery and dispatch. I'm called to attend both of these cosmic human events. But after twenty years I'm still not sure what exactly my role should be. At birth it seems I'm only there to intervene if Mother Nature falters. Death, on the other hand, simply makes me some kind of umpire – strike three, you're outta here. Could what I say make any difference? Can't someone be really dead until I give the okay? In either case there is a sense of being more a voyeur than a participant. In the delivery room I may smile and mouth inane and cute clichés, but I cannot really be part of the joy that shines in the eyes of a mother or the happiness that echoes in the voice of a father. Nor can I feel the real sorrow of a patient's death. I may be subdued and speak in hushed tones, but the tears, the visceral sadness, the almost palpable pain, elude me. I cannot feel them. I remain apart. And surely, this is better. I have enough trouble dealing with my own joys and sorrows. Am I a gatekeeper? Do I help some in and authorize others to leave? Or am I only a symbol, a small attempt to place order on the natural chaos of life and death?

Whoa! Getting much too heavy. I'm still lucid enough to realize my thoughts have all the practical implications of black holes. Welcome back to reality.

A brief stop for a muffin and tea makes me wonder what all these other early morning people are thinking. Perhaps their minds wander incoherently as well. A few journals to peruse, a few lines to write down, and then my day will begin anew.

Fatigue will be my constant companion today. Sometimes this makes me see things more clearly or at least from a different perspective. At this morning's hospital rounds I'll marvel more easily at the new life in the nursery and think briefly of this child's journey to a farmhouse in the country. I'll wonder why the palliative care patient is struggling so hard to live and why the old lady on chronic care can't seem to die.

I'll wonder, too, at my colleagues and how they deal daily with the unending onslaught of problems. I'll hope for the surgeons' clarity and decisiveness: the cleaness and precision of their world. I'll envy the psychiatrists' insight, especially their understanding of the dynamics that drive human behaviour. I'll despair at their, indeed our, collective inability to change it very much. The internists' maze of complex signs, syndromes, and therapies may make more sense today. I might never understand the radiologist, who rarely speaks but who can deliver death sentences out of pictures of shadows.

But today I'll try harder. In my tired eyes I might see them all more clearly. Despite their bravado I sense some insecurity. Perhaps they are as incomplete, as confused, as I am.

The office will be more difficult. By mid-afternoon I may have difficulty listening attentively to all the tales of woe. And certainly by late in the day I'll feel worse than most of the patients I am seeing. The return-to-work forms, the runny noses that began this morning but had to be seen today, the legions of anxious mothers, and the walking wailing of every sort will get little sympathy and less empathy.

And at the end of the day I'll perhaps reflect for a moment about the early morning house call and try to think of some answers. But I'm sure there won't be any. There will only be a sense of wonder. Eventually I'll realize that the answer is that there is no answer. The answer is not to ask the question. The answer is to sing at five o'clock in the morning day in and day out, rain or shine because that's what you're supposed to do. To make things more complex than this is to listen for the sound of one hand clapping.

I hope to make it to ninety-three. Wisdom might be what youth trades in its years for. It hardly seems a fair bargain.

Those On Whom I Depend

*Colleague: one who is associated with another
in office or special employment.*

– Oxford English Dictionary

They are people who help me to do my job and whom I help to do theirs. They come in a variety of colours, genders, and ages. Some are easy to work with and others are a pain. Some know more about less, while others know less about more but have been there so often it doesn't seem to matter; experience hath its own rewards. They are friends and sometimes strangers. They are competent and not so competent, sensitive and sometimes boorish, cruel and kind, understanding and difficult. By and large they are just like me.

Some of my colleagues have become so predictable that they verge on becoming stereotypes, caricatures of themselves. The psychiatrists whose own problems seem to have pre-selected them for their profession, the surgeons whose work is their life, the family physicians so unsure of themselves that they become triage officers, are all real. I see them often enough to recognize a recurring theme but not so often as to believe they are more than exceptions to the rule. The best ones seem to be those whom you knew in medical school. Sometimes that connection remains strong enough to mean something. It's hard to be pompous with someone whom you've seen trying to drink a bottle of beer without using any hands.

The worst are the unknown legion you must appeal to because they are on call and you are desperate. This group seems to be getting larger as I age. They also seem younger. They don't know me and sometimes don't trust my judgement. And often they ask a lot of questions to which I don't have the answers they want, or sometimes any answer at all.

My colleagues are usually helpful. Usually, but not always. I think of one in particular who never gets his secretary to take my calls and who always agrees to see my patients quickly even when he knows the referral is one of convenience: the Friday afternoon, I'm tired, insecure, leaving on holidays, or I just don't want to deal with this problem – referral. I know and I'm sure he knows. Yet I don't get hassled, belittled, or otherwise shat upon. He remains gracious and accepting. I suspect his wisdom goes beyond medicine.

Those who carry their medical school and residency attitudes and competitiveness into the real world fascinate me. They seem only to feel good about what they know when demonstrating what someone else doesn't. I guess we all do this for a while. It is after all what got us here. For most, reality eventually intervenes. But for some the epiphany is long in coming: medical knowledge may not be my most important tool; medicine is more often art than science; compassion makes knowledge humane. As in medicine so in life, maturity takes time. It comes late to some and to some not at all.

Sometimes I just don't know who to believe. The specialist's letter I got says the diagnosis was made, the treatment was given, and the patient is now feeling better and is discharged back to my care. The patient tells me that the consultant never spent more than five minutes with them, offered no explanations or suggestions, and they feel just the same. I usually nod politely and change the subject. Judge not and be not judged. I expect I get a similar review when that patient is describing my care.

And funny! How often have I chuckled at the conclusion of a colleague's letter, "Thank you for this interesting referral"? This seems incongruous coming from a surgeon seeing his one-thousandth inguinal hernia or a urologist celebrating yet another TURP (trans urethral resection prostate). How much more would I laugh at the honest approach: "Thank you for this routine, actually somewhat boring (but hey, it's my bread and butter and besides, I need the money) referral."

My colleagues are now my peers. Some of them used to be my teachers, most still are. Graduation made us equals of sorts, although I am not naïve enough to believe in this equality.

I remember an old professor of surgery from medical school so many years ago. He was the stereotypical surgeon of his day. I don't think I ever saw him out of OR greens. He had a passion for his work that I admired and wished I could muster ... for anything. He once said, "There are no new diseases, only old friends."

I seem to find something new every day: a complaint I've never heard before, an incomprehensible symptom/sign complex, a totally foreign concept of treatment. I wonder if I shall ever reach such an exalted state of knowledge. I suspect I never will.

For years he was at the pinnacle of his profession. Indeed, he became something of a legend and profoundly influenced decades of medical students and residents. In the end he was a rather sad figure, retired but unwilling, unable to leave. Perhaps having nowhere else to go, he continued to come to the hospital daily. He seemed unable to get his allotment of positive strokes anywhere else. *Sic transit Gloria.*

I think most of my colleagues are smarter than I am. Some seem to know so much more. I marvel at their understanding of multicoloured slides at continuing medical education talks and their ability to quote chapter and verse the most recent and important studies. They even know what those wonderful acronyms, like HOPE and GUSTO, actually mean. I envy their ability. (HOPE: Heart Outcomes Prevention Evaluation; GUSTO: Global Utilization of Streptokinase and Tissue Plasminogen Activator for Occluded Arteries.)

Others are smarter because they have so much more money than I do. They are investment gurus, masters of profit making. I have a kind of perverse Midas touch: all I invest in turns to crap. I have sadly concluded that I am much too busy working ever to be rich. I simply don't have the time.

Still others are smarter because they are able to work so much harder, spending more hours and seeing more patients. They seem dependent on their practices, addicted to their patients. Surely they know more than I do.

Yet others are smarter because they work so much less. They have seen the light beyond medicine. One colleague recently retired (that is, changed his mode of practice) at age fifty, to spend time climbing mountains. One day I hope to have the courage to follow his example. I envy them most of all.

My colleagues seem little different than most people I know. Perhaps they smile less and commit suicide more. They drink just as much, although perhaps more discreetly, and have all the same messy family problems that we call dysfunctional in others. Most are not smart enough to have family physicians for themselves, choosing to struggle with "curbside" consults and "professional courtesy." In other words, they call the chief of medicine at the university they attended and hope he remembers them. Emotionally and intellectually the leap from physician to patient is one we seem largely incapable of making.

We are often neurotic and occasionally psychotic or drug dependent. We are generally quiet rather than boisterous, plain rather than flamboyant, serious rather than frivolous, conservative rather than liberal. And we take ourselves far too seriously. Better that we should laugh more and analyze less.

We are richer in dollars but poorer in time to enjoy them. Catch-22 never seemed clearer. When I have the money to do something I simply don't have the time and when I have the time, I don't have the money. We all feel guilty when we are doing "nothing." More is the pity. Nothing is such a wonderful thing to do, at times.

My colleagues make my days easier and my burdens lighter. To wander daily into the maelstrom of problems that is my practice is tolerable only because they are there. I don't say thank you often or well enough. I am indebted to all those I depend on daily, or only occasionally, and ever grateful they help me through my days.

A Community Hospital

There are eight million stories in the naked city.

– Naked City – TV series 1958-1963

Thirty years ago something happened to him. It was the defining moment of his life. And now he's admitted to hospital every few weeks.

Many years ago, as a young man, he had a small medical procedure done. Complications ensued. A tragedy resulted. He hasn't moved anything below his neck for more than thirty-five years. It is remarkable that he has lived this long. But it's getting worse. The time between admissions is shorter, his stays are more complicated.

Both time and torment have made him older than his years. Moment to endless moment his reality unfolds like a play from which he has been removed. He can only watch.

His world is so remote from mine and the doors into it so narrow that I cannot begin to imagine what lies inside. Can he close his eyes and be somewhere else? Is he living another life inside his head, a life where he can walk and talk and dress himself and brush his teeth and scratch an annoying itch and go to work and visit friends and ... Are my wishes for him also his?

Most recently he's had a stroke. It was hard to tell. His speech is garbled at the best of times, but the transient facial weakness and the CT findings gave it away. He could no longer swallow the pureed food that normally made up his diet. I think he blinked "yes" when I asked him if he wanted a feeding tube. Secretly I wanted it to be "yes" so that I could feel I had something to offer.

So many years of inactivity have left him contracted and immobilized in a near fetal position. I appreciate the irony. Beginning and end. Not so different.

Yet he can still laugh. I smile as that sound greets my tortured Russian. His wife has painstakingly taught me a few words, which I mangle beyond recognition. His laughter encourages me to play the fool.

She has cared for him at home these many years. There must be a special place in heaven for her. Every day she is there. All day long, or as long as visiting hours allow, she mostly sits quietly in the gentle sunlight by the window. Occasionally she gets up, talks to him, feeds him, or cleans him, in a way that only love can explain.

She is much less than five feet tall. Her hair is short and very grey. She must be about his age, but despite a lifetime living in Canada her speech is so heavily accented I can barely understand her. For a moment I think this is odd. Then I realize he has been her world, twenty-four hours a day, seven days a week. How has she raised their family as well? Her strength and courage seem boundless.

Does she ever wonder about how her life could have been, about the "what ifs" and "if onlys" that surely come to her in dark and quiet moments? Perhaps, like the comfort fantasies we all have about winning the lottery, she plays with these ideas. But I think such introspection is at the bottom of her psychological need-to-do list. Navel-gazing is more often the option of those whose burden is light and whose time is plentiful.

Does he wonder how his life came to turn on such a small event? Does he still wonder why? Anger, denial, bargaining, acceptance. Surely the stages are complete.

As usual, more questions than answers accompany me up the stairs to my next lesson. Ms. B was admitted a few days ago through the ER. After so many years of practice I was surprised to be surprised. Food can be in the same category as drugs and alcohol. Self-destruction through eating. This is an epiphany of sorts for me.

Packing more than 440 pounds on a five-foot frame, her heart was failing and she could breathe only with great difficulty and continuous oxygen. Her mobility was limited to a few steps and she nodded off while talking to me. She said she wanted to see her grandchildren grow up and had plans for the future.

But she ate huge amounts and squirrelled away

candy bars despite being diabetic. The distance between what she said and what she did was immense and rarely travelled. No surprise there. The knowledge-action gap exists for most of us in one way or another. I told her she would die if she didn't change. She agreed, but didn't change. I don't understand the psychodynamics that drive her to slow suicide. What force, what compulsion is so undeniable? I am sad that I can do so little to help her.

More slowly now I move on to Mrs. X just down the hall, and review her chart. Another revelation. Hope dies easily. A frail emotion at the best of times, it succumbs timidly and quickly to the march of illness. And when that illness is catastrophic, the abyss at the end of hope is bottomless.

She is less than fifty years old and of sound mind. From the neck down she is seventy percent dead. From the neck up she wishes she were one hundred percent dead. It's hard not to agree. A massive stroke has crippled her. I try to tell her inspirational stories of others who have fulfilling lives after devastating events. The psychiatrist tells her most people eventually learn to cope. She finds neither of us particularly convincing. Anti-depressants are added.

Today she has to decide on the chronic care setting in which she will spend the rest of her life. There are sadder stories. But I don't know many and it doesn't help to tell them.

I move on. Next, I see a patient whom I have followed for several days. As we talk, my thoughts gain a tangential life of their own. I have a drink now and then. A glass of wine – or two – at supper, some days. And in younger, more foolish (and less painful) days, perhaps too many on occasion. But Mr. K's life is devoted to alcohol. Has been for years. No family, never had time. No job, too busy drinking. No connections other than the bar. Liver failure is in his unrepentant future. He staggers toward it without hesitation. Has he accepted this fate? Does he even have the insight to be aware of it?

His life seems simple. There is one focus, ever clear and irresistible. He is *Leaving Las Vegas* personified, although not as well preserved or as good-looking as Nicolas Cage. But this conclusion is too easy and superficial. I'm sure his life is as complex as it is difficult. Once he gets over the DTs and the nurses have cleaned him up, he is eager to leave. Phone numbers and agency addresses are given to him. They will not be used. My legal friends tell me we all have the right to make bad decisions. Of this he has made a career.

Doctors are prone to use the word dishevelled when describing street people, alcoholics, or others of "nature's noblemen," as one of my older colleagues once put it. It implies an unkempt, bedraggled appearance: hair uncombed, face unshaven, a tired body that would make clothes wrinkle. I think the word must apply to his soul as well. And then I wonder which came first, the tattered psyche or the tortured body?

I make rounds almost every day in a community hospital of almost three hundred beds. There are at least that many stories there. I try not to make judgements and strive (although often failing) only to observe, appreciate, learn, and help a little. It is so easy to dismiss a patient as the MI (Myocardial Infarction – heart attack), the bowel cancer, the post-op. Paint them by numbers and the stories often remain untold. But stop and listen, and wondrous tales emerge.

A good friend of mine says all this is too depressing. He's probably right. Yet in my more lucid moments I think I can see beyond the despair. Maybe it's my imagination. But when I look closely and listen carefully, I see a part of me in each of them and I see the strength to carry on. I don't think there's much difference between us. As I walk out of the hospital at the end of each day, "There but for the grace of God" never has more meaning.

Courage

Cowards die many times before their deaths
The valiant never taste of death but once.
– William Shakespeare

The cardiac arrest procedure was, like so many others, probably doomed from the start. But since he was a relatively young man we went aggressively through the routine. Obesity and an already long hospital stay made IV access difficult. On my second or third attempt at a venous line I finally succeeded. As I reached across the bed for some tape a sudden pain leapt into my right hand. The needle I had used on my first or second try dangled accusingly from my palm. Instinctively I grabbed it away and massaged blood from the offending wound.

Damn. Damn. Damn. It's interesting how quickly my mental focus changed from the patient to myself. Logic fled immediately, replaced by the helter-skelter reasoning of panic. My thoughts became random messages from nowhere, their obscurity only exceeded by their haste. Would my life insurance be enough? Could I continue working? What would celibacy be like?

The arrest had wound down to a predictable but pessimistic end. Our patient's heart had begun to function again, at least nominally. He had some urinary output, but no respirations, no response to pain, and fixed dilated pupils. The vent was his next step on an inevitable downward cascade that would end in a few days.

I managed to get an internal grip and wondered if more than a few seconds had passed. Had I maintained that cool calmness that I'm supposed to in these situations? Everyone was too busy to notice what had happened, and even as I mentioned it, in measured voice, I'm not sure anyone looked up to acknowledge my words. Slowly hurrying, feeling like I should be running, I made my way to the sink where I compulsively washed with alcohol and Hibitane and whatever else I could find. I did manage to refrain from grabbing a scalpel, carving an X over the wound and sucking on it desperately ... but just barely.

Make it bleed, I reminded myself. Scrub harder. It's probably already too late. I imagined malevolent HIV and hepatitis viruses speeding through my veins, setting up an inescapable course of misery and illness. I scrubbed more vigorously. Lady Macbeth would have been proud of my compulsion this night.

Irrelevant thoughts continued to inflict themselves on my beleaguered mind. This dying man had brought freshly baked bread to my office only a few months ago. I'd known him for years as he had slow-ly declined with end stage pulmonary disease and heart problems. But realistically he was as unlikely to be HIV or hepatitis positive as my maiden aunt. More recently he was growing a plethora of unusu-al bugs from his lung, including herpes simplex and MRSA (methicillin resistant staph aureus). MRSA! MRSA! I screamed silently. My panic-driven brain, already convinced that death (mine) was imminent, now felt a final over-the-edge push as I realized that this gentleman might have an MRSA septicaemia (blood infection). At least this would be a speed-ier demise than the infectious death of AIDS or the tragic liver failing encephalopathy of hepatitis. I con-tinued to be stuck on the worst-case channel.

So many decisions to be made: open or closed casket, cremation or burial. I'd miss the kids, but they were teenagers, very resilient and scarcely aware I was there at the best of times.

I sat down to review his chart. The words came into focus but my mind was elsewhere. Should I dictate a note detailing this event? Would WCB (Workman's Compensation Board) benefits apply? The hospital did have a protocol for administering prophylactic AIDS medication following accidental exposure. Reason briefly intervened. The side-effect profile of the drugs and my more rational assess-ment that the risk was low convinced my left-brain, but not my right. I had a two-hour window within which to settle this cerebral debate. I could not win. Door A led to iatrogenic illness (caused by medi-cal intervention or treatment) and unjustified use of medication. Door B led to a what if it would have helped, how bad would I feel scenario. Before a winner could be declared time ran out. The decision was made for me. No meds.

Bloodwork needed to be done. How would I approach the gathered clan requesting an HIV and hepatitis screen on the father they revered as saintly? Self-preservation can make one surprisingly callous. I did have the decency to wait until the following day.

Sleep eluded me the rest of that dark night. A milligram of Ativan brought a few hours of troubled dreams before I needed to go back to the hospital. He remained on the vent; a beating heart, a dead brain. The family, standing vigil, knew of no blood transfusions or other HIV or hepatitis risk factors. They graciously signed a consent. I felt a momentary relief before the shadows returned. No amount of logic could convince me that I wasn't already dying.

Let's see. Draw the blood today. Send it to the Public Health Lab. Today is Monday. Probably no results until next Monday. Seven days of waiting, wondering, worrying.

This week would be insufferably long. Fear is one of those things which, like the speed of light, slow time down. Consider the motor vehicle accidents that always seem to happen as if played in slow motion. Daily, constantly, the possibilities were on my mind, clouding every judgement, inserting themselves into every action, colouring every joy, displacing any other sorrow, present in every thought. What if ... What if ... What if became a mantra, an obsession. My nights were filled with deathbed scenarios (usually I was rather heroic). To whom would I formally say goodbye and how would I do it? Should I write some farewells or leave tapes, or even videos? The sublime became the ridiculous. Perhaps madness would claim me and erase all else.

All the while I tried to listen sympathetically to the usual complaints of my patients. "I'm so tired"; "I just don't feel right." Good Lord! I'm dying and you're tired. Empathy was lost. I wonder if anyone noticed. Certainly no one asked. Perhaps they were just too polite.

The stages gradually completed themselves. I bargained with God. I promised to write this account if only I could live, although now I'm not sure why God would be interested or want me to write all this down. Perhaps as penance. It made sense at the time. I denied by way of appeal to reason and statistics. Anger was brief and pointless. Acceptance was philosophically, although not viscerally, satisfying. And still I felt the same.

Years ago we used to get needle stick injuries all the time and never think anything of them. As an intern and resident, puncture wounds, scratches and scrapes, vomit, urine, and faeces were worn as badges of some bizarre rites of passage. As a practising physician they were just part of the territory. But then HIV was unknown and the hepatitis alphabet wasn't much beyond A. More knowledge has given way to more fear. I have to be afraid now. Numbers tell me that probably less than about 0.4 percent of HIV infected puncture wounds seroconvert. I take little comfort there. I shall surely be the one.

Monday morning arrives. I stop by the hospital lab on one flimsy fabrication or another and feel only slightly red-faced. "Oh, by the way, since I'm here, you don't happen to have the bloodwork on Mr. M from last week, do you?"

The clerk casually glances through some reports. I wonder if I am sweating visibly. "No. Not yet," she replies, barely interested.

"No problem," I hear myself saying cheerfully. "Maybe I'll check back later." Maybe! I amaze myself. Maybe the Pope is Catholic. Agony.

I suffer through rounds and morning clinic, trying to pass time until I can justifiably return to the lab. Shortly before noon I call. The conversation is brief, even succinct.

"Oh yeah. They came in earlier. All negative."

"Oh. Okay. Thanks," I reply in my best monotone.

Yes! Thank you, God! I punch the sky while looking heavenward and nearly fall off my chair. My life is saved. Fortunately I am alone in my office with the door closed. Enthusiasm is reborn. Depression is lifted like a veil. The eclipse is over. I am alive. I have a future.

Breath comes more easily as I begin to do some paperwork. Every thought, every emotion of the past week seems distant, ready to vanish like a card in a cheap magic trick. Have I learned nothing?

Gradually, so gradually, nagging questions insert themselves into the corners of my joy. They grow, they insist on being noticed. Why was I so compelled to appear unconcerned, strong, in control? Why wasn't I able to discuss, to express the way I felt? I chose silent suffering bravado. Why? Because I'm a male? Because I'm a physician? Because I am a male physician?

My cowardice makes me think about the real courage of others, those who are HIV or hepatitis positive and all those who are suffering, who are dying. Their heroism in simply getting up every day stands in stark contrast to my near disabling fear. I begin to realize that courage is not the absence of fear but the ability to deal with it, to carry on despite wanting to run and hide. I'm not sure I could do that. For a week it was a terrifying struggle. For a lifetime it would require strength beyond my call.

A new admiration for those with whom I spend my time – those sick and suffering I see daily – has found its way into my days. Perhaps God did have his/her reasons after all.

Goodbye

Be it granted to me to behold you again in dying.

– Robert Louis Stevenson

There is no right way to say goodbye to someone who is dying. Though you will not see them again, words come only with great effort. They become irrelevant, inadequate, stuck in that mire between thought and expression.

Most often communication with the dying is understood: implied in the omitted word, the changed expression, the forced humour, and the unexpected presence of those not usually seen at the bedside. At least I hope that it is understood.

She was fifty-seven years old when she died. Always small in stature, the illness had made her frail, weak, tired. Too easily I assumed that death would be a blessing. But that thought was mine, as one who could only watch and wait. She never expressed it. Did she want an end to her suffering as much as those close to her did to theirs?

It wasn't until twelve years after the radical mastectomy that the first metastasis appeared. At first we tried to think that the pleural effusion was infectious, a bronchopneumonia from the cold that never completely cleared that winter. Then the subcutaneous lumps began to appear, and the ribs began to fracture and the liver to enlarge, and the feet to swell. I think we both knew all along. But we played the game. I, because I knew that to acknowledge that her cancer had recurred was to remove hope of life from her world, and she, because she saw the pain in the faces of those she loved. How could she make them suffer? How could she continue her work if she was dying?

I tapped the effusion, a procedure she hated, and sent her for chemotherapy. This she also hated, but tolerated bravely. She laughed at the hair loss and joked that her wig made her anonymous and better looking than she had a right to be. Secretly, she threw up and bore the pain with more courage than either of us knew she had.

For a time she was almost well again. I wonder if she ever dreamed that she was healed. We never spoke in terms of cure, but she always seemed so hopeful, so ready to go on, that it was difficult not to be caught up in her enthusiasm for living. Faith of this magnitude is contagious.

She had been a Roman Catholic nun for more than thirty years, much of that time serving the poorest of the poor in Peru. Her life was simplicity defined and ruled by a compassionate practicality that knew no boundaries: God, family, church, work, and self, probably in that order. She seemed never to be trying to solve the big problems. For her, abstract theology was replaced by a God whose concern was for those who often had little but life itself. Her work was at the level of every man, food on the table to-day, education for tomorrow, and faith always to hold it together. The larger scale of wars, political injustice, and all the real and imagined problems I worried about seemed to her only illusions. For her there were only big victories in little battles. She would have none of moral outrage, judgement, or any grandiose philosophizing to extract good from evil in the name of God.

Indeed, I wonder if good and evil even existed for her. I think she saw only life. Perhaps she under-stood the enigma of the poor that we will always have with us. Perhaps her purpose had become not to achieve, but only to serve.

Pain was her constant companion, a cross she carried with quiet grace and uncomplaining dignity. Morphine and oxygen became her Cyrenian, easing but never relieving her burden. As with her Master before her, only death would stop the torment. And like her Master, the strength she brought to her suf-fering conveyed an uneasy comfort to those around her.

She seemed always to be trying to smile, to laugh, to shift the focus of attention that illness brings as an unwelcome guest. Those who didn't know would never guess. Those who did could only marvel at her beauty.

Once I spoke to her of dying and I asked if she

was ready. She wondered if anyone can ever be completely ready and that, yes, there was some fear. But she had tired of life as disease had made it and surely something better awaited her.

The end came suddenly and proceeded with merciful swiftness. Although I was far away on a sabbatical when she entered hospital that final time, I felt compelled to return, as if to make a last pilgrimage. This goodbye was certainly more for my sake than hers. She seemed to inspire a sort of quiet loyalty.

The hospital room was small and crowded with family. I was grateful for their presence. Any medical work here was done and having only my hand to offer I felt terribly inadequate. I could only mumble inanities like "How are you feeling?" and "You'll feel better tomorrow." She recognized me as our eyes met and I saw no trace of sadness. She was too short of breath to speak much but she did manage to smile as she pressed $450 into my hand. Haltingly she admonished me to spend it on myself, that we all deserved a little luxury.

Like most men I have some difficulty with emotions. I wanted to say that I would miss her, that her courage and strength were examples I hoped I could follow. I wish I had said I was happy to have known her, and that her life had meaning. But I didn't. The physician in me remained in control. I was unable to make that quantum leap of faith and feeling. I prayed that my thoughts were somehow conveyed and understood.

She died a few days later when, again, I could not be near. Yet I felt close and glad when I heard she had peacefully gone.

I shall miss her in a special way. Not as I would a saint whom I had never known but at whose passing I feel sadness; rather, she shall be missed as that part of myself she came to embody, that better, more unselfish, joyfully human part that is the best in each of us. God bless you, Sister, and thank you.

A Reunion

Footfalls echo in the memory
Down passages we did not take.
Towards the door which we never opened

— *T.S. Eliot*

How many ways can you divide a medical school class? I see genders, and colours, and shapes, sizes, and ages. I see different specialties and varied interests. I see those who were friends and those who were only close to each other alphabetically. Now they seem mostly colleagues and acquaintances. I see time passed and memories; twenty-five years gone in the blink of some cosmic eye.

At first I thought I would not come to this reunion. After all, it was so long ago and time is a most difficult road to travel. I barely knew many of these people then ... and now? Why would I want to spend a weekend in awkward conversation and uncomfortable situations with virtual strangers?

Yet some feeling, some vague impetus pushed me to go. It nagged at me like an unhappy wife. Curiosity? Middle-aged, angst-driven wondering? Whatever it was, it wouldn't go away.

Who were they now? How had they changed? What could I be induced to remember? Could I go without experiencing those old feelings of inadequacy, of competitiveness? Could I look at these people without seeing measuring sticks? Was the pecking order still the same? Did I care? Would anyone care? I had to go!

There were cocktail parties, dinners, lectures, and even athletic events for those ageless jocks unable to let go of that particular illusion of youth. All these provided unique opportunities for reconstruction, even re-creation of the past. We seemed to remember largely what we wanted to remember. I suspect that such selective memory is a universal phenomenon that occurs anywhere that recollection might become painful or unsure. It seems a perfectly natural mechanism, something that Freud would endorse.

Perhaps one-half of the class was there and I spoke, however briefly, to about one-half of these. It seemed a mellower, quieter, less aggressive group than I remembered – the result of age, experience, and perhaps declining hormones.

I also felt different in talking to them. I was no longer competing, no longer trying to justify my choices, no longer evaluating myself in terms of others. Had I finally found enough self-confidence, enough security? And this took twenty-five years.

Much was made of accomplishment and indeed many had accomplished much. I guess it's just
a matter of perspective. We numbered among us a
neurosurgeon, a Renaissance man who lectured easily on da Vinci and seemed to live in a different world
altogether, as far removed from mine as Brooks from
Bach. There was also an Ivory Tower (read University Centre) neurologist who walked with these kings,
yet even in our cursory conversation I could sense a
common touch. We might still be friends.

My roommate of so many years ago seemed
little changed. He has travelled the world speaking about lung transplant anaesthesia, but I see a
slightly more wrinkled, wiser Peter Pan, the frenetic
energy of youth now eclipsed by the necessary res-
ervation of age. The PAIRO (Professional Association
of Internes and Residents of Ontario) rep of long ago
continues to tilt at windmills. His activism hasn't altered, only changed address.

The closet door has opened to welcome the
millennium. Change has begot more change. I met
those with new wives and new lives. I wondered
if they are accompanied by new hopes and new
dreams. But the conversations always seemed afraid
to go there. We generally avoided anything heavy. If
it couldn't be asked, absorbed, and responded to in
thirty seconds, forget the thought. Stick to the superficial, the transcendent. Times change. People
change.

We are now colleagues or maybe just acquaintances, who shared a few years long ago and have
returned to give this time perhaps more importance
than it deserves. Then again, perhaps I am too se-

vere in my judgement. Perhaps I am still afraid, looking too deeply for too little, lost in that familiar abyss of self-doubt. Whoa! Stop that train.

I wandered from small group to small group at the cocktail party. My thoughts scattered madly. I cannot imagine the west coast hedonism of skiing over one hundred days a year. Nor do I have the courage to work in a Borneo jungle and adopt Vietnamese children. I admire the compassion and soft words of a gay activist and I am comforted by small-town G.P.s who seem to have all the same questions and lack of answers that I do. This latter group seem to exude a relaxed worldly confidence. They seem happy, content, in a real way. I admire them. But how can I know what lies beneath the few minutes that we spend together? Perhaps all is assumption.

Samuel Beckett suggested that ninety percent of life consists of just showing up. My thoughts wandered to Beckett as I sat at the Saturday President's Luncheon honouring the medical graduates of University of Western Ontario. I smiled as speeches were given emphasizing the positions and academic achievements of our medical alumni. The earliest class represented, 1928, had a table with only a few chairs occupied. I wondered if anyone spoke of their achievements at that table. I suspect just being able to show up was what they prized most.

Dinner that evening saw us gather around small circular tables in a large banquet room. People gravitated to those with whom they had associated years before, perhaps in the hope that something would be left there to sustain the evening. Conversations were at first excited, even animated. The details of our lives needed to be cleared away. But kids, work, and nostalgia didn't seem to last long. As time wore on more couples spoke only to each other. Shortly after, people began to leave, relatively early, as is perhaps befitting our age or at least our level of tolerance. How often did conversations end with hollow promises of further contact? Promises meant to facilitate easing out the door. Promises as a social convenience, never meant to be kept.

In the end I drifted away quietly, without announcement, saying few goodbyes. As I left I passed near someone with whom I had not spoken. A successful ophthalmologist – I remember admiring his basketball prowess of so many years ago. He was engaged in a conversation with a group, but as I walked by he extended his hand without turning around. I'm not sure why I was moved by this simple gesture. Perhaps I sensed (perhaps I created) a desire to acknowledge a common past and recognize an undoubtedly common future.

I realized these were essentially good people who had probably led essentially good lives. No saints and lots of sinners, but good people. People with the same problems, the same questions I have. There is really very little difference between any of us. We are a picture of everyman, going through our seasons, our lives hardly earth-shattering, mostly mundane and filled with uncertainty, joy, and sadness ... and life, precious, precious life. And I suspect these generalizations go far beyond our small group. Not exactly an epiphany, but serendipitous none the less.

In the end I felt good about going. But I also felt a sort of pervasive sadness. The necessary existentialism of living never seemed more apparent. This passage of time and evolution of ourselves is neither good nor bad, desirable or to be avoided. It simply is, as natural and necessary as morning light and ocean tides. Perhaps I came looking for heroes and villains but found only myself and was disappointed. But then realized that wasn't so bad. I'm already looking forward to the next reunion.

Who Will Whisper Vespers

Come back. Even as a shadow, even as a dream.

– Euripides

It's three a.m. when I start my car at the hospital parking lot. As it comes to life a Gregorian chant begins to play on the radio. The solemn canticle evokes a smile from me. Perhaps God is watching more closely than I thought.

In the hospital room I have just left a young man lies dying. Despite the best efforts of many he is unlikely to live until dawn. And if he does the victory may be pyrrhic beyond measure. A massive cerebral haemorrhage has demanded one outcome or the other. Medical interventions have been exhausted. Palliative morphine has delivered him to a place where he awaits the inevitable. I have brought the bad news to the family, I hope as gently as that can be done. And as I walked slowly from one darkness to another, I've said a silent prayer for the soon to be departed. The song of the monks playing on the radio seems a fitting conclusion to this early morning's tragedy.

Before I left the family I asked if they had any questions. There was silence for a moment then his wife, through a veil of tears, asked simply, "Why?" My reflex response was to say that I did not know why and that we needed to ask that question of a higher power. Quickly I realized she might be speaking of the physiologic and not the metaphysical. I retreated and launched into a complicated anatomic and pathologic account. Before I got very far she courageously mustered a small smile that stopped me. Speaking softly she said that yes, she had meant the larger "why" and she did not expect an answer. Too bad. I had a good explanation for the smaller question and none at all for the greater one.

In the few minutes' drive home, I thought of how easily and often death comes into my world. I accept this with an it-goes-with-the-territory resignation. But I think it affects me more now, a natural consequence of age and extrapolation, I suppose. A patient's death is always a humbling experience, one that rudely interrupts my agenda and reminds me that I haven't yet seen the master plan. John Donne aside, I cannot ask "for whom" each time the bell tolls. That price would be too great. I can react sympathetically, empathetically. I can care without the visceral pain of family. Care borne of the realization that another being separated from me only by luck, genes, and circumstance is suffering and dying. As often as not I can provide no medical miracle. Death will come surely, slowly, and hurtfully. I can do little but buffer the visit.

For some, I think it is a welcome release. But most rage against its intrusion. Some never get past denial. For a few there is equanimity – death as a transient inconvenience. These I wish to emulate.

My father died recently. He was eighty-eight years old. My head was ready. My heart wasn't. As convinced as I was that the death of an old man is not a tragedy, I found little solace there. More often than not, sons become their fathers, or at least a reasonable approximation. When I was young I resisted this inevitability and desperately wanted to be someone, anyone, else. Now I see this metamorphosis as natural and mostly good.

My father wept for his father. I have wept for mine. My son shall weep for me. The moving finger having writ moves on, endlessly scrolling. Not all my piety or wit shall lure it back to cancel half a line. Apologies to Omar Khayyam.

A good friend and colleague also died recently. He was a kind and gentle man. He never complained. He died quietly, courageously, even simply. I visited him, not often enough in those final days because I was more afraid than he was. His wife had died the year before. His children were grown, healthy, and had children of their own. It seemed his life was complete. Maybe this gave him a sense of readiness. He wasn't particularly religious in a formal sense but he believed in God, even if he wasn't exactly sure what that meant. His life was testament enough. If I were God I would welcome him. I mourn his loss and mine.

As I age, am I subconsciously preparing? Rehearsing, as it were, how to behave, how to react, how to accept? Trying to learn what is a good death or, more importantly, what is a good life? Vague philosophic concepts make the most sense at three o'clock in the morning. A good night's sleep will relegate them firmly to the back of the queue by daybreak.

Can I ever reach the stage of seeing death, as Karl Rahner put it, as "the unconditional, quiet, yet trustful capitulation before the incomprehensibility of one's own existence and thus also before the incomprehensibility of God"? I think this is theology-speak, for you can never know much about dying, living, or God. Most days I am content with this. But sometimes at three a.m. I still wonder who will whisper vespers over me. Who will sing Sanctus?

Too Complicated

And he, repulsed, – a short tale to make, –
Fell into a sadness, then into a fast,
Thence to a watch, thence into a weakness,
Thence to a lightness; and by this declension
Into the madness wherein now he raves
And all we wail for.

– William Shakespeare

She died. I knew she would. From the beginning I had a bad feeling that this case would come to no good end. It was the perfect storm of medical complexity, ethical morass, and legal pitfall. Solutions were always a little, or more often a lot, out of reach and problems solved always seemed to lead to more problems.

She came to the ER because her right leg was grotesquely swollen and painful. She was dishevelled, and could barely walk. A venous Doppler demonstrated extensive deep venous thrombosis. Routine bloodwork showed a severe anaemia and abnormal white cells. A bone marrow confirmed an acute leukaemia. But she insisted that someone had been threatening her, contaminating her food and transmitting secret radio messages to her.

She was just sixty years old and although she had immigrated to Canada from Central America more than twenty years before, she spoke English only in an uncomfortable and halting way. Seasonal farm work at minimal wage kept her drifting from place to place. There was no husband or significant other, no kids, and no family that she would tell us about. No friends, if any existed, came forward. She denied any previous medical contact or problems. A month prior to coming to hospital she had quit going to work and secluded herself in a rented room. Despite extensive efforts Social Services could find no one to speak for her or who knew her in more than a passing way.

Save for her demons, she was the very definition of being alone, and very sick, and probably very afraid.

Why do some people seem to have only bad luck, as if fate really was conspiring against them? Their lives become a succession of losses and all their energy is focused on damage control. But this judgement is premature. What did I really know about her?

She refused anticoagulation, cancer clinic referral, and any further treatment or investigation. Good nutrition and keeping her persecutors away was, she insisted, what was needed. I think she didn't leave hospital only because she had just enough insight to realize she couldn't walk very well and that at least here there was warmth and food, even if the intrusions of strangers would have to be tolerated.

I told her she would die soon without proper treatment. She seemed to understand, although no amount of explanation, cajoling, imploring, or pleading changed her mind. I spoke to her alone. I spoke to her through a Spanish interpreter. It didn't matter. I was never able to reach her, never able to make any connection. We were in different realities.

A psychiatric consult suggested paranoid schizophrenia complicated by acute medical problems, all of which would impair her ability to make treatment decisions. A Form One was possible, but since this patient wasn't leaving hospital, unnecessary. The psychiatrist felt declaring her incompetent and involving the Office of the Public Guardian and Trustee (OPGT) would be appropriate. Bless him; he didn't have the heart to dismiss the patient as competent and simply making bad decisions.

I called the hospital ethicist. Once the question of competency was decided, treatment decisions should be left to OPGT, he opined. Straightforward, but not particularly helpful.

I called the cancer clinic. They would see her immediately, but doubted that treatment could be given if she resisted. That is, they could not realistically restrain her chemically or physically for the four- to six-week course of potentially very toxic chemotherapy she would need. They would be happy to assess her but unless she was cooperative and willing, they could not proceed.

I tried the patient again. With a large dose of medical sophistry she did accept, for the time being, transfusion, anticoagulation, and antipsychotic medication, but she remained steadfast in her refusal of definitive treatment for the leukaemia. Some time was bought. But too many questions remained. Would the psychotropic medication provide some insight soon enough? Would she continue her on-again, off-again compliance or would she soon stop all interventions? I told her the oncologist had suggested she might live as little as six to eight weeks if she refused treatment. She wasn't interested.

There had been throughout a sort of passive-aggressive demeanour about her. She refused some treatments vociferously but when approached with an IV line for insertion, she did not withdraw her arm. Could we push this farther?

The plan became to call an ambulance, load her on the stretcher, and deliver her to the cancer clinic. There she would be assessed and treated. If anywhere along the line she began to physically resist, our plan would be abandoned. OPGT agreed to this approach. She got as far as the cancer clinic before she refused with more than words to go any further. A frustrated hematologist called and explained his position. It was too dangerous to force treatment on a struggling, uncooperative, rather large woman. Send her back if things changed – that is, if she worsens to the point she can't refuse or she has a change of mind.

Impasse: immoveable patient, and physician at wits' end. There remained a slim hope. Would her medication deliver her from the evil of her delusions before disease ended her life?

It didn't happen. She lingered on for the predicted six weeks and then died rather suddenly, never once breaking character.

Death came no easier to her than living. With no family to help with burial costs, Social Services assumed that responsibility. But they could not proceed until it had been established that no funds of her own existed. It took nineteen days for police to confirm that only the public purse remained to take her to a pauper's grave

I suspect no one went to the funeral. I didn't and for this I feel guilty as well. Guilt, that most Catholic of emotions, comes as easily as death into my world. Doubts persist. Could I, should I, have done more? Had I failed her? Had the system failed her? Had she failed the system? Had she failed herself? Had some higher power failed all of us? Or did it matter? As usual, more questions than answers. In the end, dead is dead, and maybe what is, is what is meant to be. So it goes (apologies to Kurt Vonnegut). Balm for the conscience, comfort for the soul.

The Prayer Lady, The Bomber Pilot,
and The Russian Princess

Old age ain't for sissies.

– Bette Davis

She said she would pray for me. I asked her why. She said she prayed for many people. I asked her why. Stooped and frail, she wore the lassitude of ninety-seven years as transparently as she wore the pale blue wool sweater that seemed to grow from her shoulders. I had seen her before in the hurried and harried rounds I make here. My progress notes say repeatedly, "No problems reported." But today I took the time to listen. She told me this story.

At age twenty-six she was newly married and recently moved from Ontario to an Alberta town. That same year she found a cancerous breast lump. Within a few weeks a lump appeared on the other breast, also cancer, and was accompanied by a pelvic mass. The end result was bilateral radical mastectomies and a pelvic exenteration (removal of the pelvic organs). She was crushed: disfiguring surgery, a dismal prognosis, and no chance of the children and future of which she dreamed.

It was by chance that she was treated in a Catholic hospital, although she was neither Catholic nor particularly religious. A few days after her last surgery an elderly nun – stern-looking, no-nonsense type, wearing the traditional black and white habit – visited her. They spoke, or rather, she spoke and the nun listened. Venting herself through tears and talk made her feel better. The nun said simply, "I will pray for you" and with that rose from her bedside chair and walked to a nearby window where she knelt and not so much prayed as spoke to God, as if to ask a favour of a friend. "Lord, this child has suffered much. If you will, look with kindness upon her. Ease her burden and guide her way." A few moments of silent meditation followed before she wordlessly left the room.

In the difficult journey of her recovery the prayer was soon forgotten. Some weeks later, when it was time to leave the hospital, she and her husband decided to drive back to Ontario and resettle with family. On the day of discharge the elderly nun visited again and asked her to stop in Saskatoon at the local hospital. There would be someone waiting for her. Little else was said. Just goodbye and good luck.

Depressed and overwhelmed, she hurriedly agreed, without really asking why. Some medically related checkup, she supposed.

Now, Saskatoon was only a day's drive and there were so many things crowding into her confused mind. Would her husband be able to find work in these difficult times? What would she tell her family? And how could she possibly prepare for the inevitable and probably not-too-distant conclusion of her illness?

But stop they did. A brief introduction at the hospital prompted the arrival of a nurse carrying a blanket-wrapped bundle in her arms. With few words, little ceremony, and almost no paperwork she was told, "This is for you." Into her arms she accepted a baby girl, perhaps a month or less in age. She remembered that the decision was not particularly difficult. It seemed as natural as birth itself.

They took the child back to Ontario. Her husband found work. There was no further cancer. The rest of their lives happened. And it was this daughter, now in her seventies, who was coming to take her shopping today.

She began to pray that day in Saskatoon and now she prayed for anyone who asked and for most of the people she met. Her prayers were simple, silent, and usually made from a chair beside the window in her room. She thought that sometimes they were answered and sometimes she just didn't know.

I didn't refuse her prayers. As unsure as I was what it meant to have someone pray for me, I felt comforted by the caring that was implied. Perhaps her prayer had already been answered.

* * *

The pilot is eighty-five years old now. In 1944 he was a young man and the captain of a Lancaster bomber. Mission after mission he flew over Germany. His tour included the firebombing of Dresden. He says he feels bad about it now and wished it hadn't happened. But at the time they were the enemy and he was doing his duty. With the perfect vision of hindsight he wondered if he should have been such a good soldier. He offered that blind patriotism and unquestioning obedience are too often the afflictions of youth and innocence, and that if generals actually had to fight, there would be fewer wars.

I enjoy hearing him meander through the past. He remembers engines that wouldn't quit despite bullets and fire, and adjacent planes that fell from the sky in sad numbers. He survived where many didn't. About this he often felt guilty.

As an old man he recalled all the young men and the clarity of their world and purpose. He missed those times or at least the feelings they evoked. And he remembers that he didn't pray that much except when things got really bad and then it was a reflex.

Today he tells me he still wonders why he lived through it all, had a wife who loved him, a successful career, and sons who visit him regularly. About all this he feels guilty as well. But I think the guilt is surpassed by the joy of living. He is undefeated still. In the end he has loved life too much to leave it and it seems to have loved him in return.

* * *

Today my Russian princess is having a good day. She briefly recognizes my presence and purpose before withdrawing into her world of long ago.

Her father was a major in the Imperial Guard of the Russian army, assigned to the protection of the Czar. She remembers a palace and playing with the children of privilege and she remembers meeting the Czarina. But these are the memories of an eight-year-old child filtered through the life of a woman now over a hundred years old. They are vague and grainy like old photos. Fragile, almost ephemeral, I wonder if they are a combination of the past that was and the past that she wished had been.

Sometime in 1916, her father met Rasputin, the evil monk who seemed to exert so much influence on the Czar. He knew then that he and his family must leave Russia. Stealing away in the middle of the night with only what they could carry, it took nearly two years of running and hiding to traverse war-torn Europe and arrive in America in 1918. And life blossomed anew. It will end here, where she is again an eight-year-old princess playing in the palace.

* * *

Making rounds in a chronic care setting can be dreary and depressing, filled as it is with dementia, incontinence, and regret. But if I take the time to listen, if I am not bullied by the frantic demands of work and play, then my rounds become a fascinating mosaic. I see the sorrows and joys of each long life. I see the rich history of their experiences. I am quietly moved by their stories, even those shrouded by an impenetrable veil. As I leave I feel a little wiser than before, and not as sad as I thought I would. And I see all of us, all of our journeys, all of our stories, reflected in the mirror of their wrinkles and smiles.

God

Tho' much is taken, much abides

– Alfred, Lord Tennyson

Today I met God. She was twenty years old, almost four feet tall, and nearly bald. She was also macrocephalic (having an abnormally large head) and couldn't hear, speak, or see. She did, however, possess a smile that could brighten the darkest hour. Innocence was defined in that face.

Why does she smile? Does she know? Is it possible to have insight without having knowledge? Can someone so immersed in suffering know anything else?

Her tiny body was joyously lost in a hospital bed that was acres too large. Hidden among the flowers and softness of a duvet brought from home, she seemed playful and genuinely happy. Naïvely I wondered why. One day, one day soon I think, she will not recover from a respiratory infection like this one. She will then die.

Can God die?

An attractive woman of about my age hovers at the bedside anticipating every need. This mother is life itself. She is warmth, food, shelter. She is infinite, unconditional, and painful love.

She has cared for her daughter since birth, and had long ago stopped asking the big questions. Bitterness was foreign to her and I believe she considered herself lucky. It seemed like every moment of her life was devoted to her daughter.

A grandmother sat nearby arranging tactile toys, stuffed animals, and coloured plastic rings at the foot of the bed. Does she spoil her granddaughter as a grandmother should? How do you spoil a child such as this? What could you possibly give her that wasn't deserved? What power does a child so mistreated by fate hold?

She is the same age as my children. Reflexively, I feel gratitude that they are not so afflicted. I don't think I would have the strength, the courage to go on every day. Maybe God would help me. Maybe that strength is secretly within each of us … or maybe I would turn and run. She giggles at my examination and beams a smile. I am in awe.

Today I met God. She is tiny in stature, a fifty-nine-year-old mentally challenged lady with a slack-jawed, edentulous "Popeye the Sailor" face. A basilar artery aneurysm has grown to an inoperable size and compresses her midbrain. The neurologist said she was "locked" into this level of consciousness and might remain there a long time unless surgical decompression was possible. The neurosurgeon said her chances of surviving the necessary surgery were small and even if she lived she might have horrible neurologic deficits.

Her caregivers related how she had been "not right" for almost forty years, ever since her abusive husband had murdered her father and mother while she watched and then had taken his own life. So she lived quietly enough within the security of one institution or another. No one ever visited. There weren't any children and whatever extended family existed had long since forgotten her, or had died. She was alone. They said she smiled a lot and had a sort of hesitant and apprehensive friendliness. They said she was an everlasting child in retreat from a world of pain.

The appointed public guardian suggested that since there was no advance directive all medical decisions were mine. Was I God too?

Hour after hour after day after day she lay unmoving on her bed silently challenging me to act, to make decisions. Would she want a DNR (Do Not Resuscitate order)? A feeding tube? The risk of surgery? The questions seemed too intimate, more the domain of a lover than a stranger. At her bedside I was humbled by the honour, the privilege I had been given. But was the servant worthy of the task?

She died before the issues were settled. Perhaps there was a message there. I felt relief, a sad happiness at her death and her life. But these were my emotions and I had thought that this was not about me. Now I am not so sure. In the end, simple acceptance was the necessary answer. Hers as well as mine.

I wish I had attended her pauper's funeral. How

easy it was to find excuses. The bleating demands of every day made me convince myself I was too busy. I regret this decision now. Medicine is full of regrets. She remains in a small recess of my mind. I hope I remember her. I hope I remember her lesson.

Today I met God. He was seventy-nine years old and in the process of dying; not the "natural causes" death of dwindling away quietly with the years from a failing heart or faltering kidneys, but the rapid and ugly death of cancer spread everywhere, full of pain and indignity, mocking his weakness.

He no longer functioned in any conventional reality. He only dropped in occasionally to remind us he wasn't quite ready to die, but had really lost interest in living.

Is there a place we go before dying, some purgatory that eases us more gently from this world to the next? Do some spend longer here while others don't bother going at all?

A son sat beside the bed holding his father's hand for as long as a father lets an adult son hold his hand. Periodically he became angry and struck out at whoever was near. He needed someone to blame. How easy it was to forgive this trespass.

In the end there was little I could do but provide some small measures of relief. Oxygen, morphine, and tired words were all I had to offer. I hope he took some comfort there.

Today I met God. He was a twenty-four-year-old labourer who had been married for one year and paraplegic for two weeks. A single moment of carelessness had irrevocably altered his path a million miles from any vision of the future he had ever had.

Once, on morning rounds, I found his wife in bed with him, huddled closely, trying to recreate what had been. Since then I have always spoken loudly or shuffled papers or somehow made myself more obvious before entering a curtained semi-private bed area.

They exuded defiance and denial as they faced the world. Acceptance was distant and just now, far too overwhelming. Rage seemed so much easier and appropriate. He thought he would walk again. He didn't want to believe. He kept hoping for a miracle, not recognizing the miracle that already happened.

I could teach him about catheters and wheelchair transfers, but I couldn't teach him about acceptance or resignation. Perhaps he needed the fire, the rage, to fuel the remainder of his life. Purpose is found in strange places. Perhaps it is better to not go quietly.

There is so much sadness every day, and one person wins a lottery. The natural justice of getting what you deserve is mocked. Tragedy begets tragedy. Innocents are lost. I see far more questions than answers, more despair than hope. I grow tired and confused.

And then I meet God again.

Waste

*When I give food to the poor, they call me a
saint; when I ask why the poor have no food,
they call me a communist.*
  – Archbishop Dom Hélder Câmara

The legacy of a dictator includes a children's
prison where 410 boys and girls aged seven to
fifteen exist on thirty cents a day – children whose
only crime was being an orphan, or stealing food;
children who don't know their names or where they
came from or how old they are.

This was the reality of Haiti in 1984. It may be
symbolic of the state of the nation – poor, confused,
diseased, and hungry. When President for Life Jean-
Claude (Baby Doc) Duvalier fled the country in 1986,
this change in government must have brought the
people great hope. Those at the very lowest level of
existence can only move in one direction. Yet change
would be difficult. Tyranny is too often replaced only
with more tyranny, poorly disguised as good.

In 1984, around Easter, my wife Clare and I spent some time working in Port-au-Prince with the Sisters of Charity. As a Canadian, my life has been blessed with abundance. Poverty was a distant problem. I was a stranger to suffering of the magnitude we saw. Our introduction to Haitian reality was a culture shock beyond description.

I knew that Haiti was the poorest country in the Western Hemisphere and one of the poorest in the world. Its then roughly six million people were crowded into a population density one hundred times that of Canada. Life expectancy was a long-suffering forty-seven years, literacy was optimistically estimated at twenty-three percent, and the average annual income was estimated to be $250 US. Industry was non-existent and almost everyone suffered from disease, malnutrition, or outright starvation. In 2018, Haiti ranked 168 out of 189 countries on the UNHDI (United Nations Human Development Index). I suspect that is a large improvement.

It was ironic to work as a physician in a country where the doctor who came to political power in 1957 raised brutality to levels seen all too often in the developing world. With the use of his Tonton Macoute (secret police), Dr. François (Papa Doc) Duvalier virtually eliminated the entire middle class in the 1960s. His son Baby Doc was no less despotic.

My memories of Haiti remain sharp. But the feelings evoked by being amongst the poorest of the poor fade or are subconsciously denied as being too painful. Yet these feelings are important, as words seem horrendously inadequate to describe what one sees in Haiti. The gap between seeing and describing in any meaningful way what I see of poverty, hunger, suffering, and death is one I cannot close. My middle-class naïveté tells me being poor is not being able to buy your kids a birthday gift. My eyes tell me poverty is dying. To be poor in the developing world is often to die slowly. In Haiti death is all around.

A twenty-year-old woman is admitted to Sans Fils, the Sisters' adult hospital. It is more accurately a last home for the dying. She has advanced tuberculosis and malnutrition. As I removed two litres of greenish fluid from her right lung, I thought, 'She may be dead tomorrow; she will die in a dirty, dark, crowded, stinking room in a hospital that has no nursing staff at night. She will die alone and frightened. In the morning her body will be quickly removed to make room for another.'

I admit a one-year-old boy to the Children's Hospital that the Sisters run. He weighs less than four kilograms and has severe kwashiorkor (protein malnutrition) and multi-drug-resistant tuberculosis. It is his second admission here. When discharged three months ago he weighed over six kilograms. His mother sold the medication he had been given, in order to buy food. The absolute horror of making that decision assaults my imagination. I thought he might live. He didn't. His chances really weren't that good to begin with: the mortality rate for children under five approaches fifty percent.

Even an illiterate Haitian couple can calculate that if half their kids die before the age of five, then they had better produce a lot if anyone is to care for them as they age. Children are the only retirement savings plan when social programs are non-existent.

This would seem to expose the popular North American fallacy about reducing the birth rate. Improve conditions and the birth rate will lower itself.

So children are everywhere. They seem always to be underfoot. In fact, they become a form of currency. Entrance to food lines is easier with a starving child in tow. An emaciated child can be "rented" for that purpose.

The phrase "food line" suggests the hungry get fed. But there is never enough. Malnutrition is the rule among most Haitians. We pass out powdered milk and corn to people who are starving. Our evening fare in the Sisters' guesthouse, though spartan, is more than many eat over several days.

Haiti is everywhere a land of cruel contrasts. Palatial houses guarded by high walls topped by razor wire rise over the cardboard shacks of their neighbours. One family's sewer is another's drinking well. We visited a tourist beach one Saturday afternoon. It was a lovely setting, away from the endless squalor. It cost $2.50 US to take a small boat there – one percent of the average annual income for a Haitian.

In Port-au-Prince the senses retreat from the assault of open sewers, unending din, and abject poverty. The Duvaliers' legacy to their people also includes a government that could not function without large amounts of foreign aid. Haiti has been and is a missionary vassal state existing on whatever crumbs remain after a tiny circle have lined their pockets. Corruption is rampant. Indeed Canada had cut off direct foreign aid to Haiti, terming the government a "kleptocracy." Even during my short stay this was evident. A nurse working with the Sisters was trying to adopt a Haitian baby. She was met with outrageous demands – such as a letter from the mayor of Toronto attesting to her good character – until the proper bribes were made. Electricity in Port-au-Prince was shut off every afternoon, "officially" for three hours. In reality it was usually five or six hours or more. The hydro-electric plant above the city was never completed because the money was "lost." A city of 750,000 people trying to function with no running water, no traffic or street lights, no electrical power for six hours every day. It was chaos defined. The traffic problems alone were horrendous.

Medically, Haiti is one giant incubator for infection. TB is endemic, malaria is rampant, hepatitis is routine. The smallest ulcer is an invitation to osteomyelitis. Venereal diseases of every type are widespread. And all are exacerbated by the underlying malnutrition.

One can accept, to some degree, pain, suffering, and even death. It is remarkable how callous one can become when bombarded by unending inhumanity. What I could not accept was the incredible waste of human potential, of children who would never grow up, of adolescents who would never rise above subsistence in their short adult lives, and of adults unable to achieve even the minimum needs to support their families. I was struck by this one day while making rounds at Sans Fils. A woman of twenty or twenty-one caught my attention. She had severe TB and she was dying. She had the strength to sit on the side of her bed for a while, unsmiling, proudly stoic. Her face was that of an African Queen born out of her time, ebony black and majestic – a face that could grace a magazine cover. It occurred to me that she would not live to learn of her own beauty.

I have tried to piece together what one individual can do when faced with the monumental suffering and injustice of the developing world. I have no easy answers or even difficult ones. Perhaps Mother Theresa was right when she said that we are not called upon to find answers, but only to serve. This is certainly difficult for the goal-oriented, results-directed North American mentality to accept.

So what can we do? As tired as we might be of hearing it, we can give. But give most of all our compassion. Understand that we are our brothers' keepers: we must feed the hungry, clothe the naked, and comfort the homeless. In tangible terms this means giving money, materials, or time.

If we ask why so many in the developing world are sick and hungry we should do so without fear of being labelled. Archbishop Dom Hélder Câmara of Brazil observed, "When I give food to the poor, they call me a saint; when I ask why the poor have no food, they call me a communist." Political change is essential to whatever progress is possible, and from this distance in Canada, I hope any new Haitian government would make food, clothing, and shelter its first priorities.

I returned from Haiti a bit sadder, a great deal wiser, and filled with admiration for the work of Mother Theresa's Sisters of Charity. I will continue to work in the developing world periodically and do what I can at home, all the while realizing that the only change may be in me. My skepticism is fuelled by the knowledge that politics and human nature are among the most difficult things in the world to change. Yet to abandon this challenge would be to deny our own humanity.

Escape

We are all born mad. Some remain so.

– Samuel Beckett

It is that time of early morning when the air is very still and a grey mist rises from the water to be burned off by the rising sun. The Empress of Japan stands quietly by the water's edge, looking out over the still bay, awaiting the return of her fleet. She wears a straight, shapeless dress of dull colour, rather more plain, and certainly of lesser quality, than royalty would demand. Yet she does carry a regal aloofness, an aristocratic demeanour. Presently she gives up without comment and returns to her room. No matter – she'll be back tomorrow.

He's short, fat, unshaven, and dull. Despite a history of violent rages, he's friendly in the anxious way small dogs are toward strangers: eager to please yet unable to control their excitement. After six admissions he's come to regard the hospital as a place to which he is taken when he can no longer control the demons that urge him to douse himself and the car containing his wife and daughter with gasoline. He doesn't understand self-immolation or chronic schizophrenia. He only knows he gets crazy and loses his temper. After a while he feels better. Maybe he is right. To define it any further is to be lost in a complexity that no one seems to understand.

What does a small-town family practitioner do when he's tired of the runny noses, the neuroses that never improve, the overanxious mothers, the incompetent, the impotent, and the walking wailing? A month-long locum at the Penetanguishene Mental Health Centre (MHC) seemed like a good idea. It would be my respite from the routine of everyday general practice.

The human brain may be the pinnacle of God's creation. It is simple enough to appreciate the beauty of a flower, yet complex enough to break down with alarming frequency. In any given year 1.5 million people in Ontario will demonstrate some signs of mental illness. Of these, about 38,000 will be depressed enough, anxious enough, psychotic enough to warrant admission and treatment in a mental hospital.

Almost everyone has a significant emotional stress at some point in their life. Indeed, more than ten percent of the population will eventually present to a primary care setting with emotional or behavioural complaints. As a family physician, I'm apt to spend upwards of thirty percent of my time dealing with psychiatric problems.

Statistics aside, one need only go where the money is. Bookshelves abound with self-help testaments. From Leo Busculgia's latest invitation to universal love, to Gail Sheehan's guide through the years (*Passages*) to Canada's own Peter Hanson's *The Joy of Stress*, and *Stress for Success*, there is no end to advice of both philosophic and psychiatric bias.

Now some of us carry our crosses along socially acceptable paths. Others don't or can't. They descend into some private hell, into behaviour as far beyond everyday comprehension as a magician's deceptions to the unaware. Fifteen years of general practice had not left me completely naïve. I had long since given up the quest for answers to big questions: Why do bad things happen to good people? What is good? What is evil? Why is there so much mental illness in such a prosperous society? They all seemed to have the same answer as a Zen riddle.

I would be content with smaller questions and answers that I could understand. So I went forth with lifejacket and safety net intact, secure within the rigid and protective confines of medical knowledge. To walk naked into a place of emotional nudists is not conducive to psychiatric well-being. However, too often I found my garments to be those of the emperor.

Into this mental maelstrom I plunged replete with newly gleaned textbook knowledge. I felt an old, familiar excitement unknown since the eager days of my medical youth as a student, intern, and resident. I would experience much the same bumpy ride to reality.

The MHC in Penetanguishene in 1990 consisted

of two major divisions. One, a Regional Ontario Hospital, provided psychiatric care to local counties. The other, Oak Ridge, was a unique maximum-security treatment centre that served as Ontario's facility for male psychiatrically ill criminal offenders. The combined plant (about 360 beds; 200 Regional, 160 Oak Ridge) was filled with too many patients and too few psychiatrists.

As a GP psychiatrist I would work primarily in the admissions unit of the regional centre. Here, over half of the patient population was involuntary, either APA (Application for Psychiatric Assessment) or WOR (Warrant of Remand). Psychiatric hospitals are second only to the military in the use of lettered acronyms (many of the patients were SOL). Schizophrenia, affective disorders, personality problems, substance abuse psychoses, and organic brain syndromes comprised most of the diagnoses. About fifty percent of admissions were readmissions. I don't believe this last figure is a comment on the quality of care given, but merely a fact of life.

In another time, another place, perhaps even another life, she might have been an attractive woman. She was pretty and bright. Her name had a fresh, almost wholesome quality. So why would she inject dirty water into her leg until she developed enough infection to necessitate amputation? Why would she then refuse to use her other leg or her arms until she had enough disuse atrophy to bind her to a wheelchair and make her almost wholly dependent? She was on her way to wilfully achieving functional quadriplegia. Why not just suicide?

Categorizing her as a factitious personality

disorder was in itself a long and complicated pro-cess, the diagnosis only having been reached after years of psychiatric care. I wondered what compul-sion fuelled her need for suffering. Martyrs have a cause; she had only the pain. Was she so bereft of love, or so full of self-hatred, or so needing to atone for past sins? I would never know and perhaps nei-ther would she or any of her caregivers. This "why" would not be answered.

My patients were schizophrenics, manic de-pressives, personality disorders, affective disorders, substance abuse problems, and combinations and permutations of the above (for example, schizo-affective drug abuser). They seemed out of all but chemical reach. When adequately medicated they functioned well enough within the confines of the hospital. Would they ever be able to live in the real world? Was cure an applicable term? The readmis-sion rate gave pessimistic reply.

Daily I marvelled at the dimensions of their psychosis and felt profound sorrow for the magni-tude of their suffering. What tragedy to realize in a lucid moment that you might never be able to live in the same reality as the rest of the world. Perhaps it would be better never to glimpse the other side.

A month is a very short time. A few discharges, more admissions, keeping the lid on, applying psy-chiatric band-aids, I learned more from patients than they ever benefited from me. I came to understand the essential sadness of mental illness. Despite good efforts from caring, well-meaning staff, cures are rarely found, control is a maybe proposition, heav-ily dependent on mind-numbing drugs, and relapse seems the rule. Faced with this, I appreciate the courage it takes to be a psychiatrist. It takes almost as much courage to be a psychiatrist as to confront a diagnosis of mental illness.

Not to laugh is to cry. Runny noses don't seem so bad now.

The Beginning of the End

If God were to hold out enclosed in his right
hand all the truth, and in his left hand just the
active search for truth, and should say to me,
choose, I should humbly take his left hand and
say: Father, give me this one; absolute truth
belongs to Thee alone.

– G.E. Lessing

It's ten after two in the morning. I have awakened
with the usual adrenalin rush. The only time I
used to get called at this hour was for deliveries. I
stopped doing obstetrics a few years ago, hoping
that this would slow my aging process and perhaps
improve my sleeping. Memories of restless nights
after that initial call from the delivery room remain
with me. Lying awake, I would rehearse endless scenarios for disaster. Perhaps it is prudent to be at
least mentally prepared, but it is awfully hard on the
body and soul.

Now I am called by the same floor at the hospital about a hopelessly psychotic patient who has overdosed on Dilantin and whose sedation of fifty milligrams of Librium every four hours is not enough. The psychiatric facility refused her ticket on the disoriented express (Form 1 – Application for Psychiatric Assessment) since she was still Dilantin toxic. So I am back to being awake and worried in the middle of the night. And still I can't sleep after that first call.

Thoughts come easily at this hour into a mind free of the clutter of daylight. It suddenly strikes me that death, like birth, often occurs in the still and quiet hours. I am called to certify its visit, to testify that indeed this body has shuffled off its "mortal coil." I make a show of listening for breath sounds, looking at pupils, and feeling for a pulse, but this is for the benefit of the gathered mourners. Death is usually obvious as soon as I walk in the door. It is felt as much as observed. There is usually no secret. Indeed, my role with death has long been the source of some philosophic confusion. What am I really supposed to do? I must have missed that class in medical school. Pronounce death. It sounds so solemn, so final, certainly more a spiritual ceremony than a medical task. I make official a state of being that is already unmistakable and I expedite the paperwork for those who remain.

It strikes me that I used to attend the beginning of life and now I deal more often with the end. In many ways there's not that much difference. I suspect they would both occur if I were present or not. Maybe I make things just a bit easier at both ends.

Am I an impartial facilitator, a kind of arbiter nego-
tiating a smooth passage into birth, as well as into
death? And all those thoughts occur between the
phone ringing and my getting out of bed to go to the
hospital. Sometimes insight is easy at two a.m.

Twenty-five years of general practice has left
me tired, insecure, and not enjoying medicine very
much. So many changes. The paperwork seems to
have increased substantially as well. The technology has become more complicated, more available,
and more expected. The sheer amount of knowledge
I feel I must at least be aware of is overwhelming. Patients often know more about their illnesses
than I do, courtesy of the Internet. And I no longer
understand the acronyms in the NEJM (*New Eng-
land Journal of Medicine*). Some days I feel almost
Neolithic. I am unable to fit into the new medical cy-
ber-world, too old to begin again, and still unwilling
to recognize the approach of my professional twi-
light.

Perhaps that's why I'm now sitting in a quiet
room on the grounds of the Mental Health Centre
in Penetanguishene, Ontario. No, I'm not a patient,
although the distance from here to there isn't that
great. Once again, I've taken a few weeks away from
the tribulations of my general practice, for a change
– for a rest, of sorts. So here I am looking for myself
again. Many years ago my search involved backpack-
ing through Europe. I was twenty years old then
and it was the Age of Aquarius in the late '60s. The
young and untested (and those who could afford
it) were expected to strike out on some journey of
self-discovery, like a mandatory first-year university

course, Finding Yourself 101 – An Introduction. I'm not sure what I found then. But it seemed to work for a while.

Then, ten years ago, I felt lost and came to Penetanguishene for the first time. Searching for personal order amidst the confusion of mental illness seemed an appropriate metaphor. Again it worked for a while. I became enthusiastic and actually thought that what I did made a difference. I guess I just get lost every few years and have to send out this sort of internal search party.

There are subtle and perhaps not-so-subtle signs that the time to go again is approaching. When I look forward to stopping at the three traffic lights between my home and the hospital, I become suspicious. When the thing I want most on arriving at my office is to leave, and when I never really leave because my patients all come home with me, then I will become apprehensive. And when I begin to leave a pen and paper at my bedside so that from my involuntary mental review of the day's activities, I might jot down all the things I must do before I forget, then I will become alarmed. And when I worry to the point of insomnia about the insurance forms that had to be filled out immediately "because there is no money for food" or the house call that has to be made "before it's too late," and when I look visibly older and more tired in my morning mirror, and I feel like that spot on the weather map where storms are always gathering, then, then I will know it is really time to go again.

Now I'm working a thirty-eight hour week with no call, no committees, no politics, and no insurance or disability forms. I leave at four-thirty and my day is done. I actually leave and only occasionally take a patient home with me. I have a life – a life that is not medicine ... at least for this month-long locum. I'll return soon to my general practice, to the colds and the sore throats and the terminally worried, the sick, the dying, and those for whom life is simply too much. Some will be given a band-aid of sorts, others a few words of encouragement. To most I'll just listen while they cure themselves. Some will have lives so dysfunctional and distraught that I will wonder how they manage to carry on. Others will need only a gentle nudge in a direction they already know. A few will need more than I can give. I'll listen to each as patiently and empathetically as I can and do those things I'm able to, all the while praying that I will do no harm. And I think this might make a difference, for a little while at least. Sometimes I feel so privileged to be in the position that I am. Sometimes I curse that first day of medical school. I'm forever learning about medicine and about myself. The search continues. I hope it always will. I suspect the quest is more important than the goal and that I will never really be found.

Time to Change

The longest journey is the journey inwards.
– Dag Hammarskjöld

I have been in the same family practice for over twenty-six years. I think it may be time to leave. I hate making such monumental, life-altering decisions. It's so much easier to drift along in a comfortable and familiar space. There is after all something of home in a place where you have spent so many years, something that makes leaving daunting at best and impossible at worst.

I wonder if the most confusing and oppressive prison cell is the one I call home. It confines without bars. Its walls are welcome and its barriers lie somewhere inside of me. I cannot leave without breaking down some intangible psycho-emotional borders. I cannot leave without abandoning part of myself.

But some days it's so hard to go on. Some days the frustrations seem insurmountable and the mental fatigue withering. Some days I want to get out so badly.

As I age, the practice of medicine has not become easier. That wisdom born of experience has eluded me, perhaps rendered stillborn by technology and knowledge that have increased exponentially.

The stresses of twenty-six years seem cumulative. I worry more now than when I first began. Time has taught me the many pitfalls – medical, legal, and ethical – that await any wavering judgement. I yearn for the bliss of youthful medical innocence and the certainty of the untried. Perhaps I have seen the fullness of suffering a human body and soul waits – longs – to embrace, and I am full of doubt. Some days I think we are moths drawn to a flame, so much do we seek pain.

There is nothing simple anymore. The sore throat that used to be dismissed with a "call me in a few days if you're not better" ("But, Doctor, I can never get through to you and they won't give me an appointment in a few days.") now needs an explanation of the sore throat "rules," possibly a throat swab, and a lecture on how antibiotic overuse creates superbugs. Even if I prescribe an antibiotic I do so with trepidation. Have I checked for allergies and warned about side effects? Is the patient reliable ("I remember once you gave me something that didn't agree with me.") or must I review the chart? And if the patient is a female of childbearing age, have I asked after oral contraceptive use? There is nothing simple anymore. Perhaps there never was.

The clinic in which I work used to be four physicians and a few nurses and receptionists. We were friends and neighbours. Now we are nine physicians, and upwards of twenty staff. We are colleagues. We talk occasionally in the hallways for a few minutes. We are much too busy, too focused, to have time for each other, let alone ourselves. Maybe this is the way medicine needs to be practised now.

More and more, it becomes a job. It used to be a way of life. It can't be that anymore. The science is increasingly difficult and the art is disappearing. The laying on of hands has been replaced by the ordering of tests, the clinical/therapeutic touch by the algorithm. Perhaps medicine has evolved beyond the art. Perhaps it really is a science now. And perhaps this is a necessary and natural evolution.

Increasingly I am an anachronism. Lately I feel like Job. Everything that happens seems to be bad. One calamity follows another. Patients go sour who never should. Complications occur that are rarely seen. This sounds so feeble when explained to relatives. Or perhaps it is just my perspective now, my burnout that makes me see my world so.

I used to welcome the night. It was calm and dark, warm and inviting. Immersion there provided a quiet time of dreams, rest, imagination, and escape. Issues became clearer and answers serendipitously appeared.

Now the ghosts come at night. They steal sleep and scream silent accusation. "What if," "Should I have," and "If only" are their curses. Nightly I am placed on trial and cross-examined.

Decisions. Decisions make me tired. I make far too many every day. Often I don't know if they are right or wrong. I look at a report and tell someone they have not long to live. I look at a different report and tell another all is well. I suffer too much with the one and rejoice too little with the other. They used to be something I was good at, or at least I thought I was. Is this patient really unable to work for three months following an uncomplicated broken clavicle? He says it hurts so much. The X-ray looks okay. Range of motion and strength appear normal. But he does do heavy construction work. He has no education and mouths to feed at home. And pain is such a subjective thing. How can I know exactly what he is feeling? I can't. Yet at some point I must be the judge. The insurance company demands it and insists that I am in the best position to make a decision. Should he be off work? For how long? Should he get a disability? Permanent or temporary? I don't deserve, I don't want this kind of power.

We are supposed to be egalitarian. We're supposed to guide people to make their own health decisions. So often this is the last thing they want to do, and for some it is the last thing they are capable of doing. Or is my doctor-as-god complex showing? Some of my patients, those whom I have known so well over the years, will linger with me. Perhaps those who have grown so dependent I will miss the most.

She still comes to see me regularly. She is a personality disorder. I began seeing her when she was twenty years old. She is now middle-aged. Keeping her out of jail or a psychiatric hospital has been a victory of sorts. Every week or two for the past two decades, barring holidays, she has come to my office and apprised me of what' s happening in her life.

She's graduated from one dysfunctional family to another, only slightly better, one. But she does now have the insight to realize that at least there are a few warm bodies who would ask where she was if she wasn't there. I hardly ever do anything besides listen for fifteen or twenty minutes. And she is always so grateful. I shall miss her – or perhaps I shall just miss her needing me.

I shall not miss the incessantly demanding, reason-defying, constantly complaining, list-bringing, what-have-you-done-for-me-lately, form-filling, it's-everybody-else's-fault patients who seem to plague me daily. They are my bane. They make leaving attractive.

And I shall miss some of my colleagues. They have been my lifeline in a profession that is too often solitary and unconcerned with its own. Others won't know that I am gone. I shall miss them anyway. They have been a part of every day for so many years. Like most of us (I suspect) I grossly overestimate my own importance. In my grandiose moments I wonder just how some of my patients will ever survive without my ministering. How deluded I am. On a more rational day I realize that scarcely days after I leave my name will be difficult to recall for most.

And so I must go. But where to? Perhaps I'm tired of being "just a G.P." or "a dinosaur," as one of my colleagues observed. I suspect the era of the rural general practitioner who did a little of everything is over. Perhaps this is also for the greater good. Yet I mourn the passing. Is it a sign of age that some part of me yearns for the good old days?

I feel like I need to find a niche somewhere. Niche medicine seems to be in vogue. The obesity clinics that charge exorbitantly for common sense, the men's and women's health clinics, and the travel clinics are all possibilities I consider. I have my own personal niche working as a G.P. at a psychiatric hospital. Several locums there almost have me convinced. The pay is good, the hours are great, and the extent of things I need to know about is manageable and much less stressful. And there is the overseas work I've wanted to do for so long. But do I have the courage ... for any of these changes?

I keep looking for a place from which I could watch the world end. Perhaps this is an illusion and such perfection cannot exist. So I go on with more questions than answers. And I think that perhaps this is the way it's supposed to be at the end of the day – the Zen puzzle, not the rationalist relief. So all this complaining, this late mid-life whining is *papier maché*, hardly worth the trees. If I change or don't change probably doesn't matter much. That I examine and understand the path is a win; that I show up and do my job a victory. Whether I've talked myself into doing something different or not seems immaterial. I've come to realize that outward change is an option, not a necessity. The real journey lies elsewhere.

Friendship

Friendship should be more than biting Time can sever.

— T. S. Eliot

Eric died today. He was my best friend when best friends were important. I hadn't seen him in almost twenty years, but I still thought of him often. During those quiet times when the past moves easily through my mind, he is always there.

Friendship was easier then. Time seems to have made it much harder, much riskier. Now it demands too much and gives too little. I am too busy. I am too afraid to take a chance, too tired to make the effort. So I move through life with acquaintances and colleagues. Our lives have intersected of necessity. Our kids play on the same team. We meet at the rink and ball diamond. We work the same shift. We live next door to each other. We are friends of convenience.

Eric died today. I knew he was sick and had spoken to him only a few days before. I knew the outlook was poor. That I didn't drop my daily life and go to him will haunt me always. I will regret that the bleating demands of every day kept me from the few hours it would have taken to see him one more time.

It seemed so easy. Anyone who shared the sandbox was my friend. We had the same goals, however simple. We had the same plans, however silly. We could dream the dreams of lives unlived, of all that potential untested by a harsh world. And later it became those on the same team, in the same school, in the same class, going on the same journey. Secrets were shared. Ideas, philosophies, personalities were developed. I was sure these friends would last. I was sure they would never leave me.

Eric died today. It seemed like we had been friends forever. As first-generation Canadian sons of hard-working immigrant parents, we had much in common. Expectations of achievement and the necessity of finding our own way in a world that was an enigma to parents rooted in the ways of yesterday's home bound us inexorably. Where I was quiet, studious, and almost pathologically shy, he laughed easily and often, actually spoke to girls, and seemed comfortable in social situations that would paralyze me. He was destined for a career in people. I envied him this easy facility. Where I struggled, he coasted and where I moved easily he made do. Together we rejoiced in those adolescent feelings of immortality and omnipotence. We were the "Ubermensch" without ever hearing of Nietzsche. We were Apollo and Dionysius. I thought our sun would shine forever.

There are friends. There are good friends.

And there are best friends. Of the former I have known many, of the next, a few, and of the latter almost none. These last are the kindred spirits of imagination and lore, that rare distillation of age, circumstance, and fate that brings another being to the very brink of your soul.

Eric died today. We were friends in a time of discovery, a time when important things needed to be learned, the kinds of things you wanted to learn with a best friend. How much beer is too much? What made girls suddenly so attractive? What do you want to be? Where do you want to go? How can you get there? And what does it all mean? Questions to which there are few answers. Nights after school or work were spent cruising Main Street in search of that special something to do, which never seemed to materialize. We always ended up at the drive-in restaurant talking the night away. But our joy was the journey. The solutions would remain as unattainable for us as they have for all generations.

I regret the loss of effortless friendship as I regret the passage of youth and time, with a shrug of inevitability and acceptance. Middle age finds me with no best friend. I think I have friends, usually people going in the same direction with the same amount of money. Perhaps best friends are a developmental necessity, a natural part of youth that must at some point be left behind. Perhaps when you are at the mountaintop of your life, when you have learned that most real questions have Zen answers, then, intense friendships are no longer necessary. Perhaps age makes us evolve away from the ability to be that close. So it goes.

Eric died today. A small school in a small town could not contain us. A bigger world became ours. We made it through those adolescent years and even managed to hold onto each other for a few years of university. Career, marriage, and kids tend to eliminate a lot of what seems important. Geography does the rest. We just slowly drifted apart. In our hurry to move on, too often we leave something behind.

Eric died today. I sat near the back of the church. Sunglasses hid my tears. I wept for him. I wept for his family. And I wept for the end of that time when best friends discovered the world and in all their wonderful innocence ran to it without fear. The years have brought cynicism, the death of that naïve idealism of youth. But some part of me still believes in best friends and that joyous celebration of discovery on which young men embark. I shall not go that way again. I hope my son does. And I hope he finds a kindred spirit with whom to share the journey.

Eric died today. I will remember him always.

Working Abroad

... where the sun beats,
  And the dead tree gives no shelter, the cricket
  no relief ...

                                                    – T.S. Eliot

In downtown Dodoma, Tanzania, there is a door on an antediluvian and unassuming building on the main street. It looks like most doors on that street, shabby and hanging loosely from its hinges. The day is sinfully hot and dust swirls in the lazy afternoon sun. Only some beggars move in the midday heat, attracted to my white skin in the way a desperate man clings to hope. A sign invites me to "PUSH" and enter. I step through a portal in time and move from the swelter and grinding poverty into an air-conditioned, softly lit, New Age Internet café with computer connection to the twenty-first century. The contrast is dizzying.

In Tanzania there exist many realities that are incomprehensible to a *mzungu* (foreigner) like me.

As far beyond my understanding as the Swahili I hear spoken every day, they evoke the sin and virtue, the pain and beauty that are the developing world. Most of Tanzania lies outside of that door.

In 2004, when the kids had all left home and our house was too big, my partner Clare and I decided it was time to actually do some of those things we daydreamed about while driving to work, or imagined before falling asleep, those places that we all hear calling and usually ignore. The mystique of Africa beckoned. Our empty nest and new-life psyches answered.

We knew of the Catholic missionary order, the Precious Blood Fathers and Brothers (CPPS), who have worked in Tanzania for decades. We had given a little help over the years with the purchase, donation, and collection of medical supplies and equipment. Having M.D. after my name seemed to open some doors more easily, particularly at pharmaceutical companies.

CPPS supports and operates a 500-bed hospital in Itigi, five hours by dirt road west of Dodoma (the nominal capital), in the middle of nowhere, central Tanzania. We decided it was time to visit the country we had heard so much about from Brother Anthony Canterucci, a long-time friend, who would be our host, provider, and cultural interpreter throughout our stay.

Now "Bro" is a story unto himself. He has been dividing his time between Tanzania and Toronto for more than thirty years, raising money in one place and spending it in the other. He is the energy behind the projects, a practical dreamer, wheeler-dealer, schemer, "all in the name of Jesus" entrepreneur. I admire his boundless energy and unrelenting focus on the poor. His seventy-five years mock my younger age as I try to keep up. I fail miserably.

The facts of Tanzania are simple enough. A nation, smaller than Ontario, lies just below the equator on the Indian Ocean coast of Africa and is surrounded by countries whose names form a litany of troubled headlines – Zambia, Zaire, Rwanda, Burundi, Uganda, Mozambique. Tanzania is one of the poorest nations on Earth, ranking 151 out of 173 countries in the 2002 United Nations Human Development Index. Life expectancy is a short and brutish 55 years in 2004. The epidemic HIV infection rate of about seven percent of the population (World Health Organization) may drop this figure lower. The average income is just slightly more than a dollar a day.

The economy is heavily dependent on foreign aid. Education and health care are grossly under-funded and accurately reflect the fiscal position of the government – broke. About ten dollars per person per year are spent on health care and there are less than a dozen public universities in a country of 38 million. Most Tanzanians can afford neither adequate health care nor a decent education. And poverty breeds more poverty, sickness more sickness, a cycle as old as time itself. (Although the situation in Tanzania has improved in some respects since then, with longer life spans and somewhat lower HIV death rates, the 2018 UNHDI – United Nations Human Development Index, based on 2017 data – still ranks the country 154 out of 189, so conditions there are still dire.)

Between the lines Tanzania is both subtle and complex. "Chai" (literally "tea" in Swahili, but also corruption or bribery) is a fact of life, simply accepted as a way of doing business. Never overt, it appears in the form of delay, bureaucracy, and hassling over minutiae, and disappears with the exchange of currency. Questions are rarely answered or put directly.

This is a verbal dance whose meaning always evaded me. I never learned the steps, but Bro was a master. He could pirouette through the quagmire like a Baryshnikov of bribery, more often avoiding than paying.

In Dodoma there is an AIDS orphanage operated by the Sisters of the Precious Blood. It is called the Village of Hope. I wondered if this wasn't a sad misnomer. Lying within a walled and guarded compound it has been in operation for about two years. Several small but pleasant and clean stucco bungalows on well-kept, flowered grounds each house about twenty to thirty children, ages a few months to eight or nine years old. Each bungalow has a volunteer Tanzanian couple who act as parents for the children. There are about 170 children. They attend school, are well fed, and get medical attention. They are like children their age anywhere. They laugh and play, and in particular they want to be noticed, especially by a mother. Clare is always surrounded, small hands pulling at her clothing, wanting to show her something or wanting to be picked up. The nuns fuss over every child, call each by name, and provide as much love as is humanly possible.

And they are all dying of AIDS. Every child is HIV-positive. The doctor in me knows that if you feed, treat infections, and give love and comfort, such a child will do well for at least a while. But without, or even with, prohibitively expensive anti-retroviral drugs, what is the prognosis of an HIV-positive child in Africa? I wondered if the honeymoon period wasn't nearly over and soon these children would begin to die. I felt despair and sadness at this waste of life, this loss of so much potential. Where was the hope?

How naïve I was. I thought hope needed a future, that it couldn't be only now. These children were happy, well fed, and loved. In Tanzania, tomorrow is a risky proposition at the best of times. I failed to see the miracle in their laughter today. I needed to celebrate their lives, not anticipate their deaths. My tears were misplaced. There is hope for us all in that orphanage.

Obtaining a medical history from a patient held some difficulty. An interpreter moved my questions from English (the official language) to Swahili (the language most people spoke). With luck the patient spoke Swahili. If not, it might take another interpreter to move the Swahili to tribal dialect. Medical records were kept in English. But many of the physicians were Italian-trained and conversed in Italian. I was reminded of Babel, and wondered if what appeared on the chart bore any semblance at all to what the patient actually said.

In clinic, much of the time there was no need for words. A starving infant is a starving infant in any language. A fevered child is reasonably diagnosed as malaria. And a gaunt, sickly adult is often AIDS. Every day in Africa five thousand children die of preventable causes and six thousand people succumb to AIDS. This cavalcade of sick and dying is accepted, normal. It is simply the way it is.

I see the essential sadness of Africa in a nursery school near the hospital in Itigi. A four-year-old girl wandered in off the street and shyly approached the teacher. Without tears she haltingly asked if someone there could care for her. Her grandmother had just died. Her parents were years gone from AIDS. What becomes of this child? What becomes of thousands like her? I am haunted by the image.

Lay missionaries are special people. Anna and Peter have been in Tanzania for seventeen years. Anna is a Canadian nurse/midwife who lives and works in Dodoma with Peter, her Italian-born husband. They are the day-to-day managers of the mission's water-drilling and windmill projects. For years, Anna worked in a remote village providing medical care and delivering babies in the worst conditions imaginable. They are no strangers to the tragedies that daily life brings in Tanzania. Peter is a technical genius, designer, builder, and maintenance manager. If Bro is the idea, they and others like Father Tim (American) and Paul (Canadian) are the means. I respect and admire them all tremendously. As a naïve and self-important ("if only they could be like us") North American, I expected to see another world. What I found was a different planet. Little of what I knew had any application in this developing country.

From my world of excess I feel drawn back to Tanzania. Is it guilt that moves me? Is it some vague desire to give witness, to be enraged at the hardship and inequality? Can I really contribute very much in a world I barely know? Am I an aid tourist, going so that I might feel good about myself? Hereby is demonstrated another First World trait: paralysis by analysis.

I think I'll go back without asking these questions. I'll just go and do whatever I can for whatever time I can muster. I'll keep it simple: comfort a child, hold a dying hand, and practise the best medicine circumstances allow, realizing I will change little outside of myself. And at the end of the day I won't ask if it was enough, or the right thing. That would be self-indulgent. Perhaps the question and the answer are really unimportant. A few small actions, a few small contributions are so much larger than all these words.

The End

Parting is such sweet sorrow.

– William Shakespeare

It's over now. I am no longer a family physician or "just a GP," as my kids were fond of saying. I no longer have patients to call my own. My days are finite, bounded by specific hours of work during the day and only occasional weekends. Night calls are non-existent and the telephone never beckons me to return. I've succeeded in leaving the doctor at the hospital door when the day ends. Only my thoughts, which, out of long-ingrained habit, wander back to remind me of the identity I can never truly escape.

I am a hospitalist now. We are a new species made necessary by patients with no family physicians and by doctors who for one reason or another have, in increasing numbers, relinquished hospital privileges. When these "orphan" patients are admitted, I assume the family physician role for the time of their stay. In this 230-bed acute care general hospital, about one-third of local family physicians choose not to work in the hospital and about twenty-five percent of the local population has no family physician.

The hospitalist role may require very little effort and ability or it may demand much more than I have to give. Gone are the rushed hospital rounds, hurried through, before office hours. Now I spend every day making rounds. The volume stress of never-ending numbers that want to be seen has disappeared. Patients with multiple medical problems, acute illness, and pathology I haven't seen since medical school fill my hours. Each patient requires far more time and effort than I could afford in my previous life. Generally, consultant support has been good; only occasionally have I felt like I am left holding the bag. And this may be more a reflection of my own insecurities than of reality. My GP feelings of inadequacy move me to harangue my consultant colleagues continually. I'm sure they tire of my pestering.

I now have the luxury of time. Time to talk to patients and, more importantly, time to listen. What treasures this brings. Clear and precise minds almost one hundred years old have told wonderful stories, stories of a German naval officer who transferred off the *Bismarck* just before its last ill-fated voyage and stories of a small, hawk-nosed, brooding man of nearly ninety who was "the best sniper" in his battalion, and who now regrets those lives he took so calmly.

Their illnesses become like old friends I visit over and over. Diabetes, COPD, coronary artery disease are recurrent themes. But their stories are always new, always fascinating. I listen as a child captivated by the tales of these ancient men.

Imagine having the time to discuss cases with colleagues, or even occasionally to read the latest literature about a problem without feeling guilty about the time taken. I don't easily miss those every-ten-minute appointments of general practice.

Gone, too, are the compliance problems, the follow-up appointments who never return, the abnormal lab results that must be tracked down and followed, the Pap smear recalls who refuse to answer phone calls and even letters. I am now playing to a captive audience.

No more are the patients who "had" to be squeezed in at the end of the day who turned out to have a month-old rash. The endless forms I used to see have largely evaporated. I especially don't miss those tax credit disability forms – the ones you know the patient is probably not going to qualify for by virtue of the fact they walked in and asked to have the form filled out.

My days are much simpler now. I arrive. I do my rounds. Some days I even have an afternoon coffee break, although I've not quite been able to overcome the guilt that induces. Paperwork gets done during the working hours. I do rounds again briefly before I leave. And my day is done. After-hours calls are delegated to a call group. I am in and out of patients' lives in a few days, barely remembered, anonymous. How different from the lifelong commitment I used to feel. Not better. Not worse. Just different. And that is certainly part of what I wanted.

I'm not saving the world. I expect I never did that in general practice either. But the self-flagellation in terms of time and the neglect of other things (notably family and self) made me feel like no other goal would be worthy of the effort. Now I am content to help a few and to save myself.

Am I selfish? Should I have given all, sacrificed more? Yes, I feel guilty about leaving some of my patients. There are those who will not find another family physician because of the scarcity of doctors. There are some no one else will take because of the nature of their problems. I will miss many because they are good people and friends whose lives I shared for so many years.

Where will they go now? Am I morally responsible for them? I don't know the answers. Perhaps there are none. I have opted to leave that life. I had to. I was disappearing. The need to get out was overpowering. Every morning I counted the minutes until I could leave. Now I welcome the day. I am alive again.

Where to from here? Not sure yet. This job has many appealing features but also some that remind me of why I left general practice. But I suppose that would be the case with anything I did.

Perhaps I'll stay here for a while. I like medicine too much to quit – or it's been part of me so long I can't leave without abandoning some piece of myself. The kids are gone. The house is too big. I am psychologically free for the first time in years.

There are many roads I haven't travelled. Though I may never find that ideal position, I'm glad I made the change. The older I get the less I believe perfection exists. That certainly was a lesson long in coming. This new-found sense of freedom is exciting and frightening. I look forward to the future, to the uncertainty of the future. In middle age I am young again.

Contemplating Retirement

How old would you be if you didn't know how old you was?

– Satchel Paige

I never thought it would be so hard. One day I would simply not go to work. I would spend all day doing those things I now only dream of doing. More time on the boat. Write a little more. Read a lot more. Learn about anything other than medicine. Actually help around the house. Become that handyman I'm supposed to be. The list seems endless.

Now that I'm almost there I'm getting scared and realizing how cheap talk and daydreaming really are. I have not appreciated how married I am to my work; how important to my identity is that name tag and pager I hang around my neck each morning. I feel naked without them. They tell me who I am, and what I must do. Yet they are too much with me. When I am not working I am preparing to work, thinking about work, resting so that I can work tomorrow. I am my work. That can't be healthy. Can I ever let go?

As a medical student, lo these many years ago, I remember feeling sorry for those physicians who were wed to their jobs – the surgeon who wasn't on call but missed his daughter's wedding because he went to see one of his post-op patients in the ER, the internist who was on the ward every morning when I arrived and still there when I left every night, and the family doc trying to be everything to every one of his patients. Now I fear I have become one of them. Do I exist if "Doctor" doesn't precede my name? Where did I get lost?

Most mornings I enter the hospital with a vague sense of apprehension, a free-floating anxiety. What crises today? Will the servant be worthy of the task? The challenge is always there. Inviting, stimulating, like an addiction. In the evening I leave, exhausted, and worried (what did I miss or not do today), but often with a sense of exhilaration, mostly I think at just surviving another day. If war is an addiction, then medicine is war. Every night I know how good it would be not to come back. And every morning I cannot stay away. On weekends I tell Clare I must go in to "check my mail." Do I need the small comfort of walking those halls to get my fix? Am I so desperate for the positive strokes I get at work? Am I so pitiable? Am I so hooked?

I convince myself I don't have enough money to retire. In fact, I have way more than I need (need is such a relative term) and simply less than I want. I convince myself I am too young, yet many of my peers have quit working and seem happy. I convince myself that I am necessary, but I know that the hospital and the patients are far more necessary to me than I ever was to them. And I am willing to bet that two months after I've left scarcely a soul will recall my name.

So how do I stop? Or should I stop? Should I fall over at work one day, die in the traces? Or should I wait to be shown the door? Are all those things I dream of doing so attractive only because I can't do them? Do I need the dreams more than the reality? So many questions and so few answers. At least that hasn't changed. It's easier to keep on going as I am.

Maybe there comes a time when you just know. A good friend of mine has it all planned. Six months, four days from now he will semi-retire, and sometime after that, stop all together. Even he cannot make a complete break. I did know a surgeon once who said that at age sixty he would quit. On that day he went fishing and never came back. I envy his clarity of vision and the dignity of his exit.

So I am now in a transition phase. Old enough, but not sure enough. When I am at the hospital, I wish I wasn't. When I am not at the hospital, some part of me wishes I was. I fear leaving what I know and what is comfortable. As the sirens of retirement beckon, do I have the conviction to resist or the courage to follow? The wisdom to decide has eluded me.

Maybe I need to view retirement as if I'd won the lottery. It would simply mean the start of another career. One in which I could do whatever I choose to do. Only I wouldn't get paid for it and I really have no clue what I want to do. Hopelessly conflicted, I tell myself to stop whining. Most of the world's population would be envious of my choices and the world won't stop regardless of what I do.

The debate within continues. Each day I make a different decision. Today I am leaning toward quitting work and climbing mountains instead. Yesterday I was tweaking my schedule to squeeze in a few more days at work. So it goes. My vacillation makes Hamlet look like an amateur.

Yet someday soon one side will prevail. Will I go grey-haired and shuffling to do rounds on Sunday? Or will I listen to waves lapping gently on the hull of my sailboat while I sip a fine vintage and read a book at sunset? The decision seems obvious.

Internship

It's no use going back to yesterday because I was a different person then.

– Lewis Carroll

A thousand years ago I interned at a hospital in Victoria, B.C. It was small by today's standards and had no house staff other than eight interns. Impressively, it included both cardiovascular and neurosurgery. It's gone now, replaced by a demographically demanded nursing home.

As I near the end of my medical career my thoughts occasionally drift back to its beginning. I'm not sure why. I think some days it's just comforting to imagine a younger, more able, and more enthusiastic me, to wonder at what I was able to do, or at least consider doing.

Oddly, I feel the memories as much as I see them. The exhilaration, fear, camaraderie, satisfaction, fatigue, courage, cowardice, joy, and sadness of that time remain with me despite the ever-thickening layer of years. With little effort these emotions, and the time machine of memory, take me back. I can't imagine why anyone other than myself would be remotely interested, but I will write on, gentle reader, more for my sake than yours.

I was twenty-five years old and, like most twenty-five-year-olds, thought I knew a lot more than I actually did. Four years of medical school, of learning from books, had me believing that maybe I was ready for real patients. I was convinced that I knew the latest that medicine had to offer. A B-blocker, propranolol, had replaced prednisone as the new "wunderkind" of drugs, ultra-sound technology promised to make diagnosis easy, and there was rumour of computer-enhanced X-ray tomography (CT scans). This new and exciting world was mine and I ran to it with all the enthusiasm and innocence of the newly inducted. I would have the same bumpy ride back to reality that every generation of new physicians has: patients aren't textbooks; they are infinitely more complicated.

A year of rotating internship (the College of Family Practice was not yet a reality) was to prepare me to inflict myself on an unsuspecting public. Spending a couple of months in each of the major disciplines – medicine, surgery, paediatrics, obstetrics-gynecology, and emergency medicine (that is, being the only physician in the ER) – would, along with some elective time in psychiatry, ENT, and ophthalmology, allow me to call myself a general practitioner. "Just a GP," as my kids would later remind me. And I was proud of it.

I suspect that first year after medical school

remains of particular importance in both personal and professional ways even today. It was then that I began to feel like the real thing for the first time. I could actually introduce myself as "Doctor." Staff as well as patients addressed me as such. So it must be true. Did they know how little I actually knew or how inadequate I felt much of the time? I suspect most of them did.

As interns we worked the same ridiculous hours that interns and residents always have and I expect always will. Sleep deprivation and fatigue became our constant companions but so did excitement and joy at learning and doing things of which we had only dreamed. The Professional Association of Internes and Residents of Ontario (PAIRO) was just getting started so the call schedule was largely dictated by the hospital. One in three was the rule except when on obstetrics or surgery when it was one in two. And the next day was a regular workday. We did then as others do now: we coped, for better and worse. I understand some studies have shown that morbidity and mortality rates in hospital go up in direct proportion to physician fatigue. Makes sense. Other studies have suggested that limiting physician hours does not make as much difference as might be thought as these same rates also go up with increased patient turnovers. So it goes. More questions than answers.

Much of the time we were alone in the hospital. This was most stressful when it was my one in three night in the ER. Oh, consultants would come in when asked, some eagerly and some not without pleading. Plus ça change. But mostly I felt alone. What and how much I didn't know were never more obvious. Oddly, after forty years of practice that canyon is not a whole lot smaller. The medical knowledge, technology, and pharmacology that I need to know at least something about is massive and expanding rapidly every day. Closing the gap has been a long fought and mostly losing battle. As with all generations I often learned of necessity. Fortunately, experience tempers a dearth of knowledge and makes it tolerable.

There were two other Emergency departments in Victoria then, one at the Royal Jubilee Hospital (it was larger and had residency programs) and one at the naval base in Esquimalt (which handled primarily military personnel). I wonder now if the city ambulance dispatch had an unspoken pecking order of where patients would be sent. So bullet proof did I feel those many years ago that this thought never crossed my mind. Now I think it very likely.

It was an era before central lines, CVP (Central Venous Pressure) monitoring, and PICC (Peripherally Inserted Central Catheter) lines. Long-term IV access was routinely done by peripheral "cut-downs." On my very first day on call I was summoned to the ICU to see a patient whose IV sites had all been exhausted. I was expected to do a cut-down. As anxious as I was to demonstrate my knowledge and clinical skills, I failed on both counts. The nurse did manage, although just barely, to avoid laughing out loud as in my nervousness I began to attempt a cut-down on the lateral side of the ankle of an unhappy patient. She quite diplomatically suggested that I would have more luck medially. This might be funny to anyone old enough to remember cut-downs and a little anatomy.

There was an intern's lounge on the top, fifth floor, of the hospital. It held a few worn sofa chairs, an old couch that you could sleep on if desperate, a blackboard, and a ping-pong table. A long row of windows provided a beautiful view of the city to the west. This was most beautiful in the dark and quiet of the early, early morning hours. Usually later in the day or in the evening a few of us were able to gather and commiserate. Someone came up with the idea of a "boob" list on the blackboard to record our more egregious mistakes, such as my ill-fated cut-down attempt. However, this idea soon lost its appeal and became sad. We were now in the real world. Our errors had consequences.

In-hospital acute care is an intense environment. What you do matters a great deal and if you do it for upwards of ninety hours a week some of what you see and learn is bound to stick. I remember the general surgeon who seemed to do everything from the neck on down. We joked that his notoriously brief pre-op physical examinations consisted of placing his stethoscope just below the xiphisternum and listening to the heart sounds, breath sounds, and bowel sounds all at once. He was actually a wonderful surgeon whom we all respected immensely. I remember the puzzles of internal medicine and the internist who always came in promptly when asked, cheerful and happy to teach. And I remember Psychiatry's bent at the time seemed to be Transactional Analysis and Scream Therapy. I never really understood either one. So many memories.

Of the eight interns who began that year six ended up having long careers in general practice. One died tragically young just after finishing an orthopaedics residency and one became an oncologist. I was the only one who ended up back home in Ontario, although all eight were originally from east of Manitoba. I have not seen or spoken to any of them in over forty years. Yet their young faces and personalities and the experiences of that year remain vivid. They are etched in my memory as if written in permanent marker on the convolutions of my brain.

Why have I taken to watching reruns of *Scrubs* on Netflix? Why does age demand that I review the past? If I sit quietly it returns in small bits like movie trailers of another life. I wonder if I was really there. How accurate are those memories and what drives them to resurface? Why do I need to remember? It's not like I can change anything that happened. I just relive and wonder why. This exercise produces some joy and some sadness. But I don't have many regrets, only the usual "what ifs" and "if onlys" that are obvious in the retrospectoscope. None that matter, really. All in all, it's been a wonderful ride. I can only hope the journey ahead will be as grand as the one I have left behind.

Summing Up

It's over now. My career. A large part of my life and identity for the past forty-five years. All that's left is the memories. I have only the remains of the day to fill. Right now it's hard to say just how that might work out.

My life today has fewer boundaries. I get up when I want to and stay up sometimes much too late. There are fewer places to be and not as many people to demand my attention. My limitations are not imposed by a schedule of appointments and work commitments. They are self-imposed, and often the result of trepidations about health, wealth, and the future in general. Oddly I feel, occasionally, just as busy as I used to be. Yet this "busy-ness" does not wear on me like the old days.

It's been four years since I retired and began thinking about and working on this book. I am still not totally used to my new life. For the first year after stopping medicine I dreamt about work almost every night. During that period of REM sleep I was at the clinic or the hospital, always seeing patients and always behind schedule, worried about difficult problems or questions to which I had no answers. These days such dreams are down to a few times a month. I mostly enjoy them now. They can be put into a kind of perspective that wasn't available before. That time is done.

I read and I write. I am a closet writer. Most of what I commit to paper will never see the light of day. But, increasingly, I enjoy the process. In the summer I sail the usually calm waters of Lake Erie and sometimes race around the buoys on Wednesday nights. Our three kids are scattered from Vancouver to Calgary to the U.K. We encouraged them to see the world. They took us seriously. We spend a lot of time in airports. In large part, I am content with trying to grow old gracefully with the help of family and friends.

My identity as "Doctor" is now fading. I think of myself in that way rarely. I only use "Dr." as part of my name when it might provide a little leverage, as in phoning a pharmacy to fill a prescription. In the end I loved, for the most part, my time on the frontlines of medicine – just a GP, as my kids used to say, and I cannot imagine a more fulfilling career. Couple that with a partner, children, and now grandkids, all of whom I cherish, I cannot help but consider myself among the most fortunate of men.

Acknowledgements

There are so many people I need to thank.

Lesley Choyce at Pottersfield Press took a chance on an unknown writer. Editors Julia Swan and Peggy Amirault fine-tuned my manuscript and Gail LeBlanc designed the cover.

Dr. Ross Pennie, my good friend and fellow writer, and author of the Zol Szabo Mystery Series published by ECW Press, suggested the title and provided encouragement in word and example.

Thanks to all the colleagues who made my work, at best, a pure joy, and at worst, tolerable. Special thanks to Drs. Peter Kursell, Greg Johnston, and Bob Dukelow. We worked together on a handshake for twenty-seven years.

Thank you to the Brantford General Hospital and all the physicians who made my life easier while I worked there.

I am grateful to Colin Leslie and those editors who preceded him at *The Medical Post* for publishing many of these pieces over the decades.

Thank you to Vince Hanlon for allowing me to use some of his poetry in "The Existentialism of Birds."

My high school English teacher, Arnie Stover, told me he thought I could write. He died a few years ago. I'm sorry he didn't get to read this, and to know that his influence kept me writing during those "lost" years when I struggled to put pen to paper.

A special thank you to my partner, Clare, and our three kids, Kaley, Kristan, and Kipling. This book took years to write and bring together. Always you were there with quiet encouragement and inspiration. My apologies for all the time I didn't spend with you.

Nasser Hussain, a poet and my son-in-law, and Kaley Kramer provided invaluable editing suggestions, proof reading and technical help, in that patient way that the cyber world must be explained to yesterday's generation. Thank you.

And my deepest thanks to all those patients who have made these memories.